the POWER of FORGIVENESS

Discovering the pathway to freedom

CHARLOTTE BRIGHT ASANTE

Acknowledgements

Thank you, dear Lord, for allowing me to answer the call to bring this book into fruition. To my family and friends and to you dear reader, I am forever grateful. Unbeknownst to you, I have received many insights that helped make the book a reality.

DEDICATION

To all who wrestle with the concept of forgiveness: Trouble having that conversation with God? Surely, I don't need forgiveness for that….? Or you just can't bring yourself to let go of this raw pain! This book is dedicated to you all. May God, the great architect of forgiveness walk you through. You can do this!

FOREWORD

Forgiveness is a word which everyone loves to hear until they are called upon to practically demonstrate it. There are bound to be offences in almost all relationships at some point. Such offences can be physical or emotional, causing various degrees of hurt. Sometimes the offences look deliberate from the other part and abusive in nature. In such moments the snag could be that we may think we have every right to hold on to unforgiveness, after all, you might have been treated unfairly, intensely hurt and emotionally devastated. You may seem to have a 'valid' reason to be resentful, unforgiving and holding on to anger. Yet it is in such painful moments that we are called to exhibit that communicable attribute of God, 'FORGIVENESS'.

In this book, The Power of Forgiveness, the writer, Charlotte Bright Asante, skillfully weaves through the subject and presents us with a beautiful tapestry of the nature of forgiveness. How God sees forgiveness, what forgiveness is not, what it means to experience forgiveness, pursuing forgiveness, forgiving our offenders and enfolding them, even those who hurt us deliberately, what forgiveness can and cannot accomplish in our lives and to have a lifestyle of forgiveness. Dwelling on the story of the prodigal son in Luke 15:11-32, the writer starts off by showing that, the whole issue of forgiveness, is a transaction between God and Man. When that transaction between God and Man is brokered well, then it can be extended to fellow men. We seek forgiveness from God and then extend forgiveness to men, there must be the divine forgiveness which will result in human forgiveness.

You will read in this book that unforgiveness has dire consequences for people who would want to hold on to the offences of their offenders. The critical one being that it trivializes the suffering of Jesus and ultimately disproves our claim to salvation. The clarity of expression, the elucidations of the scriptural texts and the Biblical illustrations of forgiveness that Mrs. Asante brings to the subject of forgiveness in this book makes it a must-read for everyone, young and old, men and women, believers and unbelievers alike. It is not just a book, but also a great tool that can help us mend some of our fractured interpersonal relationships at all levels. Consequently, I have no iota of doubt that this book will be beneficial to anyone who reads it. I entreat you not to just keep this copy as one of the books on your shelf but to voraciously read it again and again, imbibe the contents and let forgiveness become a lifestyle. Do not hesitate to get a copy for a friend, a working colleague, or loved one, it will help them, especially those who might have been bruised one way or the other and may need to demonstrate the virtue of forgiveness.

Anthony Owusu Sekyere Kwarteng
(Pastor)Resident Minister – PIWC Sakumono

PREFACE

Tears were streaming down his face. He could hardly make out his father's wrinkled features, but the comforting sighs and warm hands were certainly his father's. He blinked hard to stop the flow of joyful tears, but he just couldn't. 'Forgiven,' he murmured in awe. 'What a beautiful word, and what power it carried,' he thought. Once again, his mind went over the horrors of the last few months and he shivered at the thought of all that had happened. Being forgiven had opened his eyes and restored so much in him. He no longer considered himself master of all he surveyed, instead, Philippians 1:21 reverberated in his heart... 'For to me, to live is Christ and to die is gain.' Now, he could savor the thrill of being alive and forgiven and this feeling was priceless. His father was also basking in the power of what forgiveness had achieved. Oh, how he had longed for today, where his act of forgiveness would manifest itself in reconciliation. Romans 12:18 was on his mind. 'As far as it depends on you,' he thought happily, 'live at peace with everyone!'

Dear reader, oftentimes we are so hurt, angry or bitter about a sin against us, that the thought of forgiveness seems impossible. Some, after enduring cruel treatment are tormented for years by memories of their wounds and only wish vengeance on their offenders. Yet, Colossians 3:13 says 'Bear with each other and forgive one another if any of you has a grievance against someone. Forgive as the Lord forgave you,' but we gloss over it, saying, 'this isn't applicable to me, my problem is real, unique and personal.' We fail to believe that the forgiveness stories we learn about in the Bible are as poignant and as real as what we also face. The parable of the Lost Son, (Luke 15:11-32) also referred to as the Prodigal Son is an example of representation of real truths about the forgiveness process. The younger son was his own hero, despising his family and without a clue that he needed forgiveness. He came to his senses by the grace of God, and went through the steps of repentance and confession till he was free to enjoy the marvels of forgiveness. The older son was domineering, inadvertently claiming ownership of wrongs he thought were done against him and refusing to see anything else. Sadly, his pride would not allow him to possess the power to forgive and be forgiven.

With the Holy Spirit's guidance, we can receive forgiveness, become forgivers and use the lessons learned in our everyday lives. God has placed the ability to forgive in every single human being as a special dispensation for a purpose – to love. Furthermore, we forgive not only because it is a command, but also because it is an opportunity to imitate Christ. The devil has succeeded somewhat in making us believe that we do not have it in us to forgive, or that if we forgive, then we are failures. That is not the case. We can activate the special power that God has deposited in us by first seeking His forgiveness, then that power acts as the catalyst that drives us towards extending forgiveness. We cannot worship God effectively if we conceal an unforgiving heart against others nor can we serve Him fully if we refuse to let go of our own sins. Psalm 130:4 says 'But with You there is forgiveness, so that we can, with reverence, serve You.' What more, we risk being handed over to our tormentors when we do not truly forgive – Matthew 18:32-35. When we martyr ourselves by enduring sins against us without forgiving the sinner, we tend not to remember that we too have sinned against God and greatly need His forgiveness. Romans 3:23 says 'for all have sinned and fall short of the glory of God.'

So why live in perpetual bitterness over a sinner's offense against you? Why miss out on God's wonderful forgiveness by holding on hard to your griefs? In Matthew 6:14-15 we find that 'if you forgive other people when they sin against you, your Father in heaven will also forgive you, but if you do not forgive others their sins, your Father will not forgive your sins.' This latter part of the passage is what the older son in the parable was all about, where he could not see past the sins of his brother and did not have the heart to forgive. So, there we have it. It stands to reason therefore that when we do not forgive others, we cut ourselves off from God's forgiveness which He has made available through Christ Jesus. 1John 1:9 says 'if we confess our sins, He is faithful and just to forgive us our sins and cleanse us from all unrighteousness.' Additionally, we must not consider ourselves heroes when we have forgiven our offenders nor should we project our expectations on them. Instead, we must tremble at the prospect of our own unconfessed sins. Proverbs 28:13 reads 'Whoever conceals their sins does not prosper, but the one who confesses and renounces them finds mercy,' for, a person who is forgiven, is one who can be forgiving. We must remember at all times that forgiveness is not an entitlement nor a trivial matter; it is humble obedience portraying God's grace.

In The Power of Forgiveness therefore, I am eager to remind you that forgiveness is a powerful act of our own personal will in obedience to God's will. That forgiveness is a tool which God has bestowed on us to apply generously as He applies it on us. That by forgiving, we trust God to bring us our needed healing. I am keen in this book to disabuse you of the idea that when you withhold forgiveness, your pain from an infraction goes away. It does not. We are pained for a reason – so that we too can appropriate God's great gift of forgiveness and secure our reservation in Heaven. It is crucial that we understand the nature of forgiveness, the need and the way to forgive and be forgiven, and the joys of forgiveness. Let us discover the true pathway to freedom today. Get to understand the power behind a forgiving attitude, learn to express it liberally, so we can be free to serve God with all our hearts.

INTRODUCTION

Life, after all, is about relationships. We were created to have a glorious relationship with God and to experience the fruits of His nature and the full effect of His glory. Intimacy with God is how we, in all humility reflect His awesome presence. It goes without saying then, that this relationship will never thrive if forgiveness is not in the mix, and we will not be able to encounter that marvelous display of God's sovereignty. Imagine then, if the power of forgiveness was nonexistent! Forgiveness is the power that makes all the grandeur of relationships possible. Forgiveness is a wonderful expression of love that changes our whole approach to living. It is the utmost of all virtues because it showcases God's love in the greatest and most magnificent way. Its design and motivation are revealed through Jesus Christ our Lord, through whom forgiveness is readily granted, assuring us of how God's love and grace are zealously at work. Forgiveness is also a sign of strength, courage, humility and obedience.

This is why Christ willingly went to the cross to pour out His precious blood so that we could rise up in repentance to receive forgiveness, be reconciled with God and be better able to grant it too. Unforgiveness on the other hand is a very cruel prison where pride, anger and strife permanently dwell to devour our joy and consume us, and while at it, stimulate rage, bitterness and vengeance. What a vile place to be stuck! Fleeing this dreadful abode of an unforgiving heart is unattainable by our own strength. It takes hearts that listen attentively to the promptings of the Holy Spirit to achieve the power of forgiveness.

I soon found out after my decision to write on this subject matter however, that the task ahead was comparable to rocket science. Grasping all the nuances of what forgiveness really entails is no easy feat. My saving grace is that Bible is very clear on the need to always seek God's forgiveness, earnestly pursue forgiveness from man, forever grant forgiveness to those who trespass against us, continuously attempt face-to-face conflict resolution and when entreated to do so, reconcile with our offenders, and then to keep doing all this every single time. Matthew 6:12 says 'Forgive us our trespasses as we forgive those who trespass against us.' Luke 17:3-4 also says 'So watch yourselves. "If your brother or sister sins against you, rebuke them; and if they repent, forgive them. Even if they sin against you seven times in a day and seven times come back to you saying 'I repent,' you must forgive them."' Yet what of those anomalies – where the offender is unrepentant or unknown or the injury is unimaginably impossible to deal with? Do we still have to forgive, and do so readily? Yes, we most certainly have to begin the forgiveness process internally, and when the sinner rises up in repentance, the entire process of forgiveness will be complete.

Forgiveness implies that an injustice has been done against us and we recognize our inability to remedy the violation ourselves so we choose to let go of the pain by allowing God to take over. True forgiveness deals with personal conflict fighting deep within us, demanding an immediate reaction the moment the affront strikes, and that can be a very arduous task on our souls. It is important to understand that the need to forgive befalls to test us. The question to forgive or not to, immediately imposes itself on us when we are wounded, and it wrenches severely at our hearts and minds, challenging us at that moment of impact. With no light-bulb moments nor audience suggestions to pick from, we are compelled to decide on what to do when the force of an offender's trespass hits us. In the eyes of God however, we always have to make the positive choice of embracing forgiveness – yes always. Does this even sound possible? You may say No, but with God's grace, we too can learn to forgive absolutely and gain the power to keep doing so. How, you ask? Well, forgiveness is a fundamental test of our humility and obedience. 1John 1:9 says, 'if you confess your sin, He is faithful and just to forgive you and cleanse you from your unrighteousness.' In the Luke 17 and 1John scripture quotations above, one says 'If they repent' and the other, 'If you confess'. 'IF'. If in all obedience and humility, we accept and act on what these verses say about forgiveness, we can have it and we can grant it too. God has forgiven and stands ready to enfold us. We too must forgive and stand ready to reconcile with our offenders, as stated above. We meet God at the point of our forgiveness through repentance and we also meet our offender at the point of their repentance through forgiveness, and then marvel at the joy this brings. When we have humbly and obediently experienced God's forgiveness, it bolsters our hearts in such a way that we cannot bear to continue hating others or harboring grudges in our hearts. Such feelings become very wretched and we no longer strive to extend forgiveness too.

In The Power of Forgiveness, let's take a scenic journey through the phenomenon of forgiveness. We will be accompanied mainly by Jesus' parable of the Lost Son found in Luke 15:11-32. This parable, often referred to as the Prodigal Son is the third in a trilogy of parables, taught by Jesus Christ in the Bible book of Luke chapter 15, in answer to the accusation of the Pharisees and the Scribes who murmured that Jesus 'receives sinners and eats with them.' – Luke 15:2 Jesus uses these three parables to illustrate how He came to reconcile Himself with sinners, and the joy resulting. In the third parable – the Lost Son, Jesus goes a step further to describe the beauty in forgiveness and how it can lead to grand scale reconciliation and restoration. All the elements of how one reaches the point of total forgiveness are woven perfectly in this parable. All through The Power of Forgiveness therefore, we will peer into the hearts of the characters in this parable and examine how their attitude and mindset draws a picture of unforgiveness, illustrates a perfect sketch of forgiveness and paints a portrait of reconciliation. What could their deep sentiments have been, and how did their thought processes impact the different actions each of them took? We will allow our imagination to run wild in an effort to understand the intricacies of forgiveness from this family's point of view.

Our journey with the characters of this parable will take us through the causes of and need for forgiveness, how to approach forgiveness and steps to take when faced with the call to forgive. We will make a stop to review the reasons why we must pursue forgiveness and at the crossroads of extending forgiveness, we will check the reasons why we must stand in readiness to enfold our offenders. Certainly, there are rough bumps on this journey that we have to carefully study to avoid. Difficulties in forgiveness will be given a hard look, then goals will be addressed with the help of the characters in this parable. We will examine reconciliation possibilities and the need to do all we can to avoid being thrown to our tormentors – Matthew 18:34. We will then make a U-turn back to study the joy of forgiveness so we are encouraged to keep on forgiving.

In Part one; what really is forgiveness? We examine the nature of forgiveness - its meanings, and how God uses forgiveness to draw us close. What drives forgiveness, and since it is a decision of our own wills, we must be careful to know what forgiveness cannot do so that we do not fall into the trap of the enemy, for subtle is the devil's best style. We will learn how the father in our parable is able to deal with his pain while choosing to forgive entirely. This father helps us to understand how forgiveness can accomplish a heart of worship and ensure ones' reservation to Heaven. Do we sometimes feel indignant that our offender will go unpunished so we refuse to forgive? How about that side of us that withholds forgiveness in order to be considered a hero or a martyr? Can that be measured as a product of pride?

Still forging a pathway to understand the phenomenon of forgiveness, Part two focuses on the steps needed to seek forgiveness. Forgiveness is the greatest measuring rod of Christian love; thus, it is in our best interest to learn the steps to seek God's forgiveness. We learn how, by surrendering in total contrition, repenting and submitting in humility, God forgives us of our sins. He expects us to seek forgiveness from our victims too and as we do, God provides us with peace and joy, conveying to us that forgiveness is essential to our eternal salvation. The truth of the matter is that forgiveness should not be limited to offenses by others because pride, self-righteousness, self-indulgence, rebellion and self-importance are all self-sins against God that need forgiveness. The older brother in our parable story helps us get a clearer picture of hidden sins that need forgiveness. Proverbs 16:25 says 'there is a way that seems right to man but will lead to death.' Our own works and abilities will not lead us into Heaven. We need Jesus who paid for all our sins on the cross. Thus, a forgiving attitude is God's expectation of us His beloved in Christ and we must learn how we can acquire that.

In the Third Part we concentrate on how we can extend forgiveness to others. We learn that we must have a forgiving disposition and a desire to grant forgiveness with all our hearts at all times. It is only God who truly wipes the slate clean, that is, purge the grievance entirely, Mark 2:7b says 'who can forgive sins but God alone?' With that in mind, we do our part in releasing all sins to the cross of Jesus and setting the offender free. The father in our parable, discharged the animosity in his heart long before he embraced his prodigal son. Often times, our human nature wants the person who hurt us to pay or suffer, but we will learn from the father in this parable that granting forgiveness is the way to go. He never once ignored the enormity of the grievances of his sons, on the contrary, he faced them squarely yet chose to forgive them all. We have no reason to wait for those who do us wrong to appear first. We take that bold step to make the connection. It may after all sometimes be that, our offender does not even know they hurt us. We must, when possible, attempt to face them with their affront as Jesus suggests in Matthew 18:15, because a relationship that could potentially be saved will be destroyed forever if we do not. We then discover that the evidence of our own forgiveness from God is when we also freely forgive our offenders and secure our place in Heaven. We will take a good look at compassion since it is key in extending forgiveness to others. Though an impossible feat to achieve by our own strength, when we show compassion by the grace of God, He gives us the ability to free our hearts from the pain enacted on us, and if need be, reconnect with our offenders.

In the Fourth and final Part of this book, we summarize everything learned about understanding and applying forgiveness in our everyday lives. We establish that forgiveness is simply God's perfect plan to teach us how to love! We fully appreciate that once we forgive our offenders whole-heartedly our own confession and repentance of sins to God will never fall on deaf ears. We also learn about the bounteous joy in forgiveness and finally with the help of our parable, the Lost Son, we identify our very stance on the voyage of forgiveness. Do come along on this journey with me and let us learn how we may always respond well to our sufferings for scripture says in 1Peter 3:9 'Do not repay evil with evil or insult with insult. On the contrary, repay evil with blessing, because to this you were called so that you may inherit a blessing.'

The Parable of the Lost Son: Luke 15: 11-32 (NIV)

11 'Jesus continued: "There was a man who had two sons.
12 The younger one said to his father, "Father, give me my share of the estate.' So he divided his property between them.
13 "Not long after that, the younger son got together all he had, set off for a distant country and there squandered his wealth in wild living.
14 After he had spent everything, there was a severe famine in that whole country, and he began to be in need.
15 So he went and hired himself out to a citizen of that country, who sent him to his fields to feed pigs.
16 He longed to fill his stomach with the pods that the pigs were eating, but no one gave him anything.

17 "When he came to His senses, he said, 'How many of my father's hired servants have food to spare, and here I am starving to death!

18 I will set out and go back to my father and say to him: Father, I have sinned against Heaven and against you.

19 I am no longer worthy to be called your son; make me like one of your hired servants.'

20 So he got up and went to his father. But while he was still a long way off, his father saw him and was filled with compassion for him; he ran to his son, threw his arms around him and kissed him.

21 "The son said to him, Father, I have sinned against Heaven and against you. I am no longer worthy to be called your son.'

22 But the father said to his servants, 'Quick! Bring the best robe and put it on him. Put a ring on his finger and sandals on his feet.

23 Bring the fattened calf and kill it. Let's have a feast and celebrate.

24 For this son of mine was dead and is alive again; he was lost and is found.' So they began to celebrate.

25 "Meanwhile, the older son was in the field. When he came near the house, he heard music and dancing.

26 So he called one of the servants and asked him what was going on.

27 'Your brother has come,' he replied, and your father has killed the fattened calf because he has him back safe and sound.'

28 "The older brother became angry and refused to go in. So his father went out and pleaded with him.

29 But he answered his father, 'Look! All these years I've been slaving for you and never disobeyed your orders. Yet you never gave me even a young goat so I could celebrate with my friends.

30 But when this son of yours who has squandered your property with prostitutes comes home, you kill the fattened calf for him!'
31 "'My son,' the father said, 'you are always with me, and everything I have is yours.
32 But we had to celebrate and be glad, because this brother of yours was dead and is alive again; he was lost and is found.'"

PART A
THE FORGIVENESS
TRANSACTION

God's heart is one of love, alien to any form of sin. He uses the process of forgiveness to display His love and nurture our relationship with Him. The forgiveness transaction is essentially a pact between God and mankind. The Bible clearly instructs us to repent of our own sins, confess it to God who will faithfully forgive and cleanse us – 1John 1:9. We can then activate the other side of this transaction which is the relationship between us and our offenders. Matthew 4:14-15 says 'For if you forgive other people when they sin against you, your Heavenly Father will also forgive you, but if you do not forgive others their sins, your Father will not forgive you your sins.' We cannot consider seeking or extending forgiveness without first approaching God. In the forgiveness transaction therefore, we seek our own forgiveness from God and extend it to others. Divine forgiveness, then human forgiveness. This beautiful transaction is cyclical in nature because God desires to have a loving, relationship with mankind. Romans 5:8 says 'But God demonstrates His own love for us in this: while we were still sinners, Christ died for us.' We cannot expect God's forgiveness if we refuse to seek it in repentance and if we also refuse to forgive our offenders. As we keep on forgiving those who hurt us, we receive God's own forgiveness. We approach God with a broken heart and humility then we pass the pardon on in the form of gratitude and compassion. We may be blinded, hurt or angry but we must never lose sight of God's willingness to forgive us. Now let us throw in a monkey wrench to cloud matters. What if those who offend us are unaware of the need, or are unwilling to be forgiven? Well, we just maintain our side of the transaction and release the offense to the cross of Jesus as we stand ready for reconciliation. While they may not be ready or able to repent of their sins, we have discharged the debt nonetheless by passing it on to Jesus. On the cross at Calvary, Jesus took possession of all our sins. Why? Because of God's grace and His heart of love. 'For God so loved the world, that He gave His one and only Son, that whoever believes in Him shall not perish, but have eternal life.' – John 3:16 We then by extension, learn how to forgive just as He forgives.

The mystery of forgiveness cannot be quantified because it is not an object that is passed around to announce its commission. Neither should forgiveness be seen as a quid-pro-quo transaction of 'I forgive you, then God forgives me.' It is so much more than that since a lot of heart is involved. As we push towards forgiveness, reconciliation may or may not occur, but at least we are set on the path of compassion and release, which is what forgiveness does. We have no fears that an infraction might occur again and our boundaries may be re-violated because we leave the possible effects of forgiveness and reconciliation to God. Society might even frown upon our willingness to forgive, but we do not have to worry about losing face or fear to offer forgiveness again and again. These are ploys from the enemy to stop us short from experiencing the marvels of forgiveness. These feelings are prideful and have no place in the forgiveness transaction. The transaction is based on the love Christ teaches, which embodies humility, trust and obedience. Let us now examine the nature of forgiveness, how God sees forgiveness, the drive to forgive, what forgiveness can and cannot accomplish using the parable of the Prodigal Son – found in Luke 15:11-32 of the Bible. Only after learning the full spectrum of what forgiveness is can we understand the joys therein.

CHAPTER ONE
THE NATURE
OF FORGIVENESS

If anyone had told him his day would end this way, he would adamantly have said that they were out of their mind. This father had certainly not seen this coming. Yet here he was, biro in hand, proficiently dividing his estate so that his impetuous son could have his share. 'Give me my share of the inheritance! Really! Where did I fail him? Why would this restless soul slight me this way?' These thoughts run through the father's mind as he mournfully did his son's bidding. His anguish was obvious to all, yet father considered the morning exchange an extremely important turning point in his and his younger son's lives. The culmination of all he had learned about forgiveness was upon him, and he knew it was a day of great testing. Was he going to be able to model God's love and mercy in the face of such insubordination? Absolutely, he vowed in his heart. He was not going to confront his son in anger because he was determined to see beyond the sin. He had conferred with the Holy Spirit and was now filled with the needed compassion, courage and mercy to offer forgiveness, because his prodigal son desperately needed that grace. Father therefore worked feverishly and equitably, dividing, separating, allotting and ensuring that his property was properly divided. Though he faced the loss of a cherished relationship with his son, he put on a brave face, allowing God's love to shine through him and with a deep breath he let go of the trauma warring in his heart. Gone was the human impulse to fight. Gone was the budding grudge that had been making its way into his heart. He reflected unswervingly on God's abundant grace and mercy upon his own life and now it was his turn to extend forgiveness. He would not fail; it was the least he could do, in the face of such mercy from God. With a determined smile, he inwardly separated the horror of the sin from his son and left it at the feet of the Almighty. Hallelujah! Forgiveness had revealed her affable face, and it was a beautiful sight to behold.

I. The Essence of Forgiveness
'To err is human, to forgive divine.' Alexander Pope1

Forgiveness is a phenomenon that we will all need to confront one way or another, as long as we are alive. Whenever we feel the need to forgive, we must be grateful because it is a good step towards receiving God's dispensation of grace. Though we may not feel gratitude initially, when God opens our eyes to notice grace and mercy very hard at work behind the scenes, resolving the wrongs done against us, we then experience the resulting joy and thankfulness of the effects of forgiveness. From being lied to, cheated, abused, broken, betrayed, stolen from and the list goes on, sin against us can be so grievous and almost unbearable. It may also be a fleeting misdemeanor that can be brushed aside – and not dealt with. Some may be able to deal with seemingly difficult situations better than others, yet whatever the case, or wherever a person may find himself or herself on the forgiveness scale, we must always yearn for and push harder to apply forgiveness properly. So, what is this forgiveness, that is mentioned well over a hundred times in the Bible?

Unfortunately, the English word 'forgive' does not satisfactorily describe the entire meaning as intended in the Bible. Forgiveness is much more than dictionary definitions which generally are to grant pardon, to cease feeling resentment against an offender, to stop feeling angry towards a person or to grant relief from a debt. Words such as to excuse, cancel or pardon are often cited to help define forgive better. These definitions from dictionaries are good, but they certainly limit the magnitude of the work forgiveness has to do for you and I. It will also be inadequate to focus on root words and origins from different languages to explain the profundity of forgiveness. Root words such as the Latin 'perdonare,'2 which means to give up whole heartedly or without reservation, or the Greek 'aphiemi,'3 which largely means to forsake, put away, send forth or remit, then there is also the Old English 'forgiefan' 4 which means to grant or allow, as well as the Aramaic derivative of 'shbakn' 5 which means to free, untie or loosen from a restraining hold, all depict the different nuances of the word forgive.

What God does with forgiveness is much loftier than any dictionary can expound. Just begin to imagine words such as separating, sending away, rejecting, overlooking and forsaking. What is common to all these distinctive facets of forgiveness is the notion of a load in motion. Stay with me now! We begin to form a sense of what God intends with the word to 'forgive.' A load in motion or the transfer of a load suggests moving matter from one place to another. Understand this movement as one made with some violence and begin to think about the process of hurling this matter away with some force as in flinging something far from you in rejection. Now work your thoughts towards giving this matter up with finality and then begin to imagine God's relationship with sin. God cannot under any circumstance dwell with sin, yet He loves us. What to do? Separate the sin from His beloved with a ferociousness so that the sin will not stick back on us but will be removed entirely and permanently. To fling sin off, hurling it away from us! To give it up totally. To for-give then simply means to 'let it go completely and hard.' To give back the relationship before the sin occurred! This is what God does when we rise up to Him with a broken heart over our sins. He has set forgiveness in motion already, so when we meet Him at the point of repentance, He flings the sin away from us and replaces it with love. Psalm 103:12 says 'As far as the east is from the west, so far has He removed our transgressions from us.' This is our God hurling our sins vehemently away from us so that we can have a personal relationship with a Holy God. This is God forgiving us. This is God wrenching us away from the ugliness of sin. Afore the sin, He gives love, gives peace, gives freedom. Forgiveness.

We obviously cannot pardon sins the way God does, but we are commanded to forgive our offenders regardless. Matthew 6:14-15 states that 'if you forgive others their transgressions, your Heavenly Father will also forgive you, but if you do not forgive, your Heavenly Father will not forgive you your sins.' Jesus set a perfect example on how we can forgive in a way that will please God and cause our own sins to be forgiven. Unlike God who can actually expunge sin by cleansing it in the blood of Jesus – Ephesians 1:7 'In him we have redemption through his blood, the forgiveness of sins, in accordance with the riches of God's grace,' we do our forgiving by 'giving' the sin to Christ and not holding the incident that caused the falling out against our offender. Consider this interesting way of looking at human forgiveness: As definition implied: forgive is two words put together. For and Give. Now, 'for' is used as a prefix just like 'pre' and means 'ahead of.' Thus, we give love ahead of the sin. Giving it from the heart, and this is an internal or spiritual activity. Then the second part of the word 'give', would be to give love face-to-face, and this is an external process. Got it? An example of forgive therefore would be Joseph in the Bible, who gave back love 'for', ahead of his brothers showing up in Egypt, where this was done deep in his heart. Then he gave back love 'give', again by reconciling with them face-to-face and showing them his heart. Also, the father in our parable, did the 'for' part of the word forgive long before his son's return from a distant country – a deep internal release, then when he saw his son coming back in the distance, he run to him and did the 'give' part of forgive, that is, outwardly showing his love by reconciling joyfully with his son. Yet another easy way to understand the word forgive is to see it as 'for' the sake of peace, I 'give' you love ahead. Or, 'for' the purpose of expressing gratitude to Christ for His work on the cross, 'give' back.

This is what to forgive literally means, to give as before... give love as before, give attention as before, give normalcy as before. We become loosened or untied from the past and offer ourselves as afore the offense. This can be achieved if we determine to allow the Holy Spirit to help us. If the offender is unknown to us, we can still exercise the 'for' and 'give' strategy by separating the sin from the offender 'for', and releasing the debt to God 'give'. From all these examples, we understand that to forgive then is to be pre-incident or afore the offense. To 'give' before! Letting the relationship between us and our offenders be one of before the offense. This is purely an internal endeavor that can spill out to the physical in the form of reconciliation. Like Jesus, we must have a heart of compassion, love, obedience and humility seasoned with prayer to be able to achieve this forgiveness transaction. More so, we must also regard the work He did on the cross on our own behalf, forgiving us of our sins. This is the inspiration we need towards setting others free, and releasing them from their debt of sin. Matthew 5:7 says 'Blessed are the merciful, for they shall receive mercy'

What then may cause the need to forgive? Betrayal, murder, denial, lying? How can we really justify our definition of forgiveness? How can we give as before or 'profess' the incident did not happen? Forgiveness is about eliminating the expectation that our offender owes us anything. The offender cannot fix the hurt within us, so we release that hurt ourselves to set us free. The offense has nothing to do with our ability to forgive. Remember what Jesus said about forgiving seventy times seven in Matthew 18:22? This is a precursor of the state God wants us to be in permanently. This may sound unrealistic and stressful. Nonetheless, with the power of the Holy Spirit, we can do this. We can reduce the trauma of the offense by asking God to help us separate sinner from the sin. Forgiveness entails detaching the horror of the sin from the one who caused it. Only then can we focus on restoring the relationship with the sinner, knowing that God will deal with the sin. This is how we employ forgiveness. As such when we refuse to take offense, we have practiced fore-giveness. If we let go the sin 'ahead of the sin,' then there is nothing to forgive after the fact, and the inevitable pain of the crime is lessened or nonexistent. This is what Christ wants for us, so when we fail to 'fore-give' we are left with the fallout of irreconcilable differences and the pain and suffering that goes with an unforgiving heart. There is a French saying 'Tout comprendre, c'est tout pardoner' – to understand all, is to forgive all! Understand that our own sins have been wiped clean and we can pay it forward. This is what the father in our parable did so well. He remembered and understood his own forgiven state and forgave his prodigal son.

Friend, these descriptions are not to detract from or belittle painful events that cause us harm. It may be a very trying ordeal, yet true forgiveness will know to detach an offender from that inexcusable wrong done for the sake of Jesus Christ. True forgiveness does not ignore, deny or trivialize the severity of the sin, but as it regards the sin, a concerted effort is made to release the offender from that burden. True forgiveness remembers God's grace when an infraction strikes, and so is able to separate the sin and relinquish it to the cross as it releases the sinner from the load of the sin. True forgiveness is when we resolve in our hearts to obey God by not allowing an offender's exploitation to dictate our own action or attitude in a negative way. Forgiveness is what God does best to lay bare His heart, and He teaches and encourages us to lay ours bare for our offenders too. He lay bare His heart by sending us His best to atone for the sin. We lay bare our hearts by sending our worst to Him on the cross and releasing the sinner from guilt. Let us now look into the workings of the forgiveness transaction and see how it fashions a lasting loving relationship with God and our neighbors.

II. The God Factor
'This is my blood of the covenant, which is poured out for many for the forgiveness of sins,' - Matthew 26:28

It is very important to state that God is the majestic pioneer of the wonder of forgiveness. It is His very heart to forgive His beloved and teach us not only to seek His pardon but to pursue forgiveness from our neighbors and grant it as well. We find our forgiveness in God's New Covenant of grace, Jesus Christ the mediator, who shed His precious blood on the cross at Calvary to save mankind. This is the foundation of the promise of God, the ultimate solution to our hapless sinful condition. Prior to the work of the cross, young animals were sacrificed to atone for sins. Exodus 24:8 says 'Moses then took the blood, sprinkled on the people and said, "This is the blood of the covenant that the Lord has made with you in accordance with all these words."' Praise be to God, that the blood of animals is no longer required for the forgiveness of sin. This Old Covenant served its purpose of providing a sacrificial system that temporarily enabled the people to remain in fellowship with God. With the blood of Jesus, there was no longer the need to adhere strictly to the Mosaic law as a counter to absolving sin. In Jeremiah 31:31, we read '"The days are coming," declares the Lord, "when I will make a new covenant with the people of Israel and with the people of Judah,"' God's heart was set on a permanent solution for forgiveness of sin, hence the promise and fulfilment of Christ's work on the cross. Hebrews 10:4 says 'It is impossible for the blood of bulls and goats to take away sins,' so it was replaced by the New Covenant. Hebrews 7:27 explains how Jesus Christ died once and for all, creating a new covenant with us, by the shedding of His precious blood for our salvation and remission of sins. 'Unlike the other high priests, He does not need to offer sacrifices day after day, first for his own sins, and then for the sins of the people. (Jesus) sacrificed for their sins once for all when He offered Himself.' This permanent solution for salvation and forgiveness of sin was God's initiative and He promised that He would be merciful towards us and remember our sins no more. 'For I will forgive their wickedness and remember their sins no more.' – Hebrews 8:12 Now, since we were created in God's own image, we too have this heart of forgiveness. To exercise the right to forgive however, it is important that we recognize our own brokenness and desperate need for God first, repent and receive forgiveness, then from our new posture, go forth and do likewise.

The point of forgiveness therefore is twofold. First to show us God's unconditional love for humanity and His abhorrence of sin. Secondly, to teach us the need to mimic God by loving unconditionally, and hating sin. God is able to separate the crime from the criminal, pardon the sin entirely and love the sinner. Forgiveness therefore, is always an opportunity to display grace, and God is keen that you and I will understand this process well. He searches for us, finds us and draws us close, while dealing with the sin for what it is. Most of the time however, when we need to forgive, our vision is badly skewed. In our wounded or guilty state, we look at the sin, the offender and self all jumbled together. Now our goal as Christians who desire to learn the power of forgiveness is to take our eyes off the sin, the offender and self and look only to God, to help us achieve this goal of true forgiveness. The moment we try to look at sin through human analytical lenses, the process will become difficult. We just have to cultivate the forgiving nature we inherently have, and leave the absolute pardoning ability to God.

In the parable of the prodigal son, the father displayed forgiveness through compassion when he saw his son approaching. He was devoid of all resentment. He had emptied himself of all bitterness and was ready to renew his love relation with his son. Luke 15:20 says 'So he got up and went to his father. But while he was still a long way off, his father saw him and was filled with compassion for him; he ran to his son, threw his arms around him and kissed him.' Long forgotten was the despair of troubles this boy had put him through. The sleepless nights and the persistent aches and worry were a thing of the past too. Such is grace. This is the forgiveness transaction taking shape. God forgiving ahead of time, restoring you and I to a great position. Are we able to rise up to the occasion and be reconciled with Him? Mention must also be made of God's grace in the transaction. His grace that flows during the forgiveness act is His love in motion. In the parable of the unmerciful servant in Matthew 18, Jesus describes the servant who knew God's grace and mercy but refused to pay it forward. The forgiveness transaction does not work that way. Matthew 18:28 says 'He grabbed him and begun to choke him. "Pay back what you owe me!"' This is how this unmerciful servant treated a fellow servant who owed him very little as compared to the humongous debt he had been forgiven minutes earlier. He did not seek for forgiveness with contrition so he promptly forgot the grace shown him, and was not appreciative. This forgetful attitude is what we have to work so hard on. We have to apply forgetfulness differently from how we normally do. We quickly forget the grace God daily bestows but that should never be the case. Is that how little we regard God's love for us? God's forgiveness yearns to teach us that forgiveness should be all-encompassing. Ephesians 4:32-5:1 'Be kind and compassionate to one another, forgiving each other, just as in Christ God forgave you. Follow God's example, therefore, as dearly loved children and walk in the way of love, just as Christ loved us and gave Himself up for us as a fragrant offering and sacrifice to God.' If we refuse to forgive as God forgave us, we are breaking the transaction cycle. Ephesians 1:7 records that 'in Him we have redemption through His blood, the forgiveness of sins, in accordance with the riches of God's grace' We have to forgive in order to allow God to forgive us and keep the forgiveness transaction in motion. Thus, we do it as He does it — ahead of time, promptly, fully and with no looking back. Now how best do we learn something if we do not actually experience and practice it? As long as we are alive, we will face the need to forgive and be forgiven. It is our burden to gaze at the forgiveness granted us on the cross at Calvary, so that we too can forgive and receive even more grace.

The forgiveness transaction is therefore an important process set to advance the love course and increase our blessings. 1Peter 3:8-9 puts it all into perspective 'Finally, all of you, be like-minded, be sympathetic, love one another, be compassionate and humble. Do not repay evil with evil or insult with insult. On the contrary, repay evil with blessing, because to this you were called so that you may inherit a blessing.' Friend, see where we are going with this? Forgiveness is therefore a very powerful phenomenon that cannot be taken for granted but should be applied at every opportunity, for therein lies our blessings. Let us master the power of forgiveness and radiate God's true image, which is love.

III. The Prodigal Son: A portrait of Humanity
Luke 15:11 'Father Give me my share….'

The pride that dripped from the younger son's demands must have been mind-blowing to his father. Whatever happened to 'please' and 'thank you' that had been drummed into his heart when he was much younger? He had been taught godly principles from the time he was a little boy. So, what happened? Where was this haughty attitude coming from? Could it be peer pressure, demands from society? Social media? Effects of single parenthood? This condition of the prodigal son is what we all unfortunately portray one way or another. His attitude describes society today. A sinful place, a miserable dwelling, a state of leaving the grace of God and proceeding into a distant country to be our own master. A society where wealth and possessions are taught to be the only requirements for a good life. 'Give me my share' the younger son demanded. 'My share' implies that he no longer views the inheritance as a gracious future gift from his father. Suddenly it is a debt owed him. That is typical of humanity. The knowledge of this inheritance had become common to him, thus was not respected. That is how we treat the grace of God. This is us: proud, conceited, self-sufficient, egoistic, can do better than God attitude. Humility becomes unfamiliar territory. We are masters of all we survey, spitting on the goodness of our Father. With this baggage, how do we in faith learn repentance and forgiveness, and how do we learn to be forgiving too? Scripture tells us in 1Timothy 6:6 'but Godliness with contentment is great gain.' At the beginning of the story, the prodigal son was not content, nor godly. This boy was almost ruined by pride. He was precarious and impatient as well as distrusting of his father. He did not see the need for a relationship with him, and was prepared to move to a distant country to waste his life away. Conceit was his middle name because he thought he could manage his possessions all by himself. He had the audacity to address his father flippantly, and how untoward is that? Yet are we any different? Has ego taken over completely? Do we not think we are proud, showing God what to do? Planning our personal trip to that distant country to squander His gracious gifts all by ourselves? We are no different. We keep pushing God away and doing our own thing and by so doing, it becomes impossible to learn the virtues of forgiveness, what more, practice it.

To rub in his disrespect, the younger son probably taunted his older brother and the servants with his new-found wealth, bragging about his trip to the distant country and boasting about the unscrupulous way he was going to waste his inheritance. Luke 15:13 says 'Not long after that, the younger son got together all he had, set off for a distant country and there squandered his wealth in wild living.' In his heart, he had already killed off his father. He had no use for him. He trusted his own schemes and abilities. This is the height of pride, and forgiveness is a very hard thing to come by in this setting. The forgiveness transaction cannot be discharged if there is even a hint of pride. Something had to give. To receive the blessings of God, a forgiveness transaction had to ensue, but the stakes were high. God demands humility, obedience, confession and repentance in the transaction, and we need God's forgiveness so we are not handed over to our tormentors. We also need to freely forgive our own offenders too for the cycle to progress.

The prodigal son was pulling no punches, forgetting that his sins had to be accounted for somehow. The proverbial 'willful waste makes woeful want' comes to mind at this point. In Luke 15:14 we see that 'After he had spent everything, there was a severe famine in that whole country, and he began to be in need.' Our prodigal son's misery was evident. He had disposed of God's goodness in a vile manner and was at the point of destitution. He did not realize the grace upon him, until he lost everything. He had hit rock bottom. Sometimes, it may take that kind of a state of being to bring us back to our knees, before our loving Father, who is standing ready to enfold us compassionately. Have you wandered from the faith in pursuit of worldly gratifications? In the book of Ecclesiastes, chapter 2:11 Solomon said 'yet when I surveyed all that my hands had done and what I had toiled to achieve, everything was meaningless, a chasing after the wind; nothing was gained under the sun.' Worldly pleasures take us away from God and His forgiveness and strains our relationship with friends and family.

We are all in need of forgiveness. Sin is sin in God's book. The severity of this prodigal son's sin is similar to what we face now. Maybe selfishness and self-will have turned us away from God and loved ones. Or maybe we are comfortable with our 'little sins.' No need to bother God with this or that! Maybe we believe we can hold on to a grudge or two because we are just not ready to forgive. If so, the meaning of the forgiveness transaction is still lost on us. It is time we saw the error of our ways. Time to repent and seek God's forgiveness. Matthew 6:14-15 says 'For if you forgive other people when they sin against you, your Heavenly father will also forgive you. But if you do not forgive their sins, your father will not forgive your sins.' We truly need to shudder at our own sins, and 'come to our senses' just as the prodigal son did, and listen out for Holy Spirit, who sees our desolate state and lifts us up. May we always see ourselves in need of forgiveness and be quick to confess and repent, so that our Heavenly blessings will abound.

IV. The Older Brother – A Heart of Stone
'For this people's heart has become calloused; they hardly hear with their ears, and they have closed their eyes. Otherwise they might see with their eyes, hear with their ears, understand with their hearts and turn, and I would heal them.' Matthew 13:15

The older brother in our parable from Luke 15 seems to have it all. Strong, hardworking, heroic, noble, wealthy and popular. He has never harassed his father in anyway before. He obeys him impeccably, and works tirelessly for father, to ensure that business always thrives. He wakes up early every day and treks to the field to labor until evening. This older brother is courteous to the servants, often having a banter or two with them. He cannot identify with the Matthew 13 verse above about callous hearts and being blind or deaf. No, he hears what he wants, sees what he likes, is kind and loving. He did not need healing he thought. Or did he? He knew the Bible verse that said 'For all have sinned and fall short of the glory of God' – Romans 3:23, but surely, that did not apply to him?

This fine sunny day seemed different though. He was not sure if it was his father's extra loud prayers for his younger brother from the roof-top, or rumors about the spread of the famine from the distant country. He remembered that a neighbor's servant had been welcomed back home after suffering adverse reaction from pig pod ingestion due to that severe famine, but that was not his problem. He felt something vast, almost spiritual was about to happen. His thoughts shifted to his younger brother as it did from time to time. 'That prodigal fool' he muttered under his breath as he drew closer home. 'What came over him? Why would you demand your inheritance when you were doing perfectly alright?' he pondered. Now chances of him getting his fair share of anything was in jeopardy. Surely their father had been bitten hard by the turn of events and he would not be surprised if father decided to give his remaining wealth to the widows and orphans before he died. That would be a big blow to him, he thought. 'No, that could never happen,' he mused. He would go on 'slaving' for that father of his, maybe father would notice his hard work and reward him. As for his younger brother, sometimes he hoped the boy would just never return so father would eventually leave everything else to him, after all he was older and better suited, he thought.

As we discover more about the older brother in the parable of the prodigal son, the scripture that comes to mind is Mark 7:21a: 'For it is from within, out of a person's heart, that evil thoughts come.' We notice that a person's true disposition is often hidden in his heart. When everything is calm this older brother is a very appealing, lovable person on the surface, but his temper and anger always gets the better of him when he is distraught. In his distress, he displays his evil thoughts, his cold heart and unlovable nature. He wants to be the life of the party always. As he nears his father's house that fateful day, he begins to hear the straits of music, and we are finally introduced to the unappealing, unlovable version of him. He cannot for the life of himself fathom why his father would make such a fuss over his younger brother. He must have hurled out all the insults he could think of and flatly refused to join in the celebration. He was very upset that this prized fattened calf had been killed for that celebration. The older brother was determined never to have anything to do with his younger brother – who he believed had brought disgrace upon the entire family. With these malicious thoughts, the last thing on the older brother's heart was to enter the home to celebrate with his family. He was aware of the Luke 17:3 verse which says, 'If your brother or sister sins against you, rebuke them, and if they repent, forgive them.' Yet in his anger, he was not prepared to do any such thing. Further, he did not think his younger brother deserved forgiveness anyway. To him, this prodigal's appearance had nothing to do with forgiveness, but everything to do with scamming their father again. No way would he attempt forgiveness, he thought, he was not going to play that 'game'. He preferred to wear his grudge as a badge of honor. What is our take away from this brother? It is immediately evident that the forgiveness transaction is not in motion in the heart of the older brother. Much as God is ready, with extended arms to forgive and enfold this lad, he is blind to that possibility and until his heart is captured by the Holy Spirit, the cycle of forgiveness cannot ensue. We learn here that some by nature, will generate any number of excuses – to avoid admitting to sin. Our narcissistic older brother does not think he has a heart of stone. 'The heart is deceitful above all things and beyond cure. Who can understand it?' – Jeremiah 17:9 Our hearts have the ability to hide us from the reality of what we truly are spiritually. 'For if you forgive other people when they sin against you, your Heavenly father will also forgive you. But if you do not forgive others their sins, your Father will not forgive your sins.' – Matthew 6:14-15

So, after a hard day's work, coming home to the ruckus of a celebration for his wayward younger brother was too much for older brother. He refused to accept the call of his father and refused to come to his senses. Luke 15:30 says 'But when this son of yours who has squandered your property with prostitutes come home, you killed the fattened calf for him!' This 'son of yours' was his way of taunting his father that he wanted no part in his brother's life nor in the homecoming celebrations. Older brother preferred to let his bitterness take root and fester in his soul. He had closed his heart to the possibility of extending forgiveness. He resented the idea that his younger brother had 'come to his senses' and was alive again. He could not fathom that concept himself, and would have preferred if they all stayed in their graceless state. This older son had taken the entire forgiveness transaction for granted. He was in his own pig-pen, but he did not realize that he was in danger of actually eating the pods of the pigs and suffering intensely from unforgiveness. How can such a soul enjoy the marvels of forgiveness? Though he did not travel to a distant country to squander his inheritance, the older brother was also squandering his life away with his sanctimoniousness and anger. He was as estranged as his younger brother, in hatred, a hardened heart and hypocrisy. His inability to enter the house to join in the celebration showed his disdain towards his father for throwing the party, and disdain for his brother for even coming back. He was estranged because of his own complacency. He was just as much a lost son as his younger brother had been. Indeed, he was oblivious to the situation, but this older brother was also hungry and lonely, contemplating eating the pods of the pigs by his show of contempt over his father and brother. He was in position for a renewal and needed the Holy Spirit to arrest his heart and help him rise out of his pig-pen. May we allow Holy Spirit to capture our hearts so we can recognize our sinful state, then work hard on pursing and extending forgiveness.

CHAPTER TWO
THE DRIVE
TO FORGIVE

Forgiveness can be characterized as a spiritual whiff that God has breathed into every human heart for the special purpose of promoting a divine relationship with Him. We approach forgiveness with joy, because the Holy Spirit continually stirs our hearts to pursue it. As we apply this God-given essence abundantly, we set the stage for an overload of God's mercy. We join Him in His passion to bring His beloved to restoration. At times, however extending forgiveness to an offender may feel even more painful than the actual sin we suffered and yet, because of this charge bestowed on us by God, we feel no peace in us without forgiveness. The reality is, unless we let go and allow God, unless we forgive our offender and forgive ourselves, until we forgive the situation and trust that the condition is over, not necessarily physically, we cannot successfully move forward, and the forgiveness transaction will be out of order. Therefore, since we are driven to forgive, we simply must obey the command to do so. We trust God through the process and He shields us from the perils and limitations of forgiveness.

I. Forgiveness is a Command

'Our forgiving others is not a cause of God's forgiving us,
but it is a condition without which He will not forgive us'
-Thomas Watson6

What is this drive to forgive? Why do we forgive? Jesus Christ is the best and only example of why we must forgive. God created humanity to develop a close relationship with Him through Christ. As stated in the Introduction, any relationship can only be maintained if the spirit of forgiveness is evident and practiced. The drive to forgive is consequently in the fabric of humanity, since we are made in God's image. This is manifest throughout scriptures. When we repent, He forgives us and charges us to do likewise. In Acts 17:30, God commands that we repent of our sins and turn to Him. Our capacity to forgive is therefore a command and not an option for Christians. Matthew 6:15 tells us that 'if we do not forgive others their sins, your Father will not forgive your sins.' Yes, that is the reality. This is a God condition passed down to us. It is boldly stated and God never instructs us to do something that He knows we cannot do. I would even go as far as stating that the act of forgiving is a calling that we all potentially have. How do we express it? Not by our own power nor our might, but the Holy Spirit who helps us to succeed.

It is our Christian obligation therefore to allow the Holy Spirit to help us master the art of forgiveness. No matter which step of the forgiveness ladder we dwell on, we ought to push harder and climb further. God sent His son Jesus Christ to shed His blood for mankind, the ultimate forgiveness transaction. By repenting and receiving His forgiveness by faith, we can do likewise for our neighbors. It is our duty to release others from blame totally and leave their infractions in God's hand. Then and only then can we truly worship God with all our might. Colossians 3:13 admonishes us to forgive as the Lord forgives. His part of the forgiveness transaction is already complete, now He commands us to do likewise. Refusal to forgive therefore is sin. When we ask God to forgive us but are ourselves unforgiving, how can we expect to receive forgiveness? How can we even have the audacity to ask God for forgiveness when we refuse to forgive? We become slaves to bitterness when we refuse to forgive. Mark 11:25 says, 'But when you're praying, first forgive anyone you are holding a grudge against, so that your Father in Heaven will forgive your sins too.' We see here that forgiveness is a prerequisite to ones' own forgiveness. It is in our own best interest to do so and quickly. In essence, forgiveness is about us, not someone else, and is something we have to experience on a daily basis.

When we consider the father in the parable of the lost son, we are amazed at the zeal he shows in his desire to forgive his son and reconcile with him. He realizes that there is only one option if he wants a relationship with his son. He took the reproach of his younger son and made it his own. For our own good, we are required to seek forgiveness and extend it. This command helps us to stay forgiven, makes us prayerful and puts an end to our suffering. It is important that we remember this mandate at all times. We are required to forgive because the forgiveness transaction is perfectly sufficient in its ability to teach. Forgiveness teaches us to love, to be caring and compassionate, selfless and most of all, to have a relationship with our Lord. We often hold on to resentment hoping to cajole our offender into admitting their wrong. We want to prove the facts of the case to the world and we like to hold the sin over our sinner's head. However, if we let go of every pre-conceived idea we have regarding when to, why, who we must forgive, and just concentrate on outright forgiveness as and when it arises, we receive our freedom to pursue our love relationship with God. Furthermore, as we forgive our offenders, we practice and imitate Christ's love and this helps us to become more like Him. This command is a very challenging prospect that requires some heavy lifting, but with God's grace and the help of the Holy Spirit, we can abide by this charge and be successful in receiving the good it has to offer.

II. Forgiveness: An Act of Obedience
'When he came to His senses, he said, how many of my father's hired servants have food to spare, and here I am starving to death! I will set out and go back to my father and say to him: Father, I have sinned against Heaven and against you.'
-Luke 15:17-18

When our young antagonist came to himself in the parable of the Lost Son, he chose to be obedient to God's call. Obedience is not always easy and this prodigal certainly found it difficult to return to his father in obedient repentance prior to his encounter with God. God however always has a plan of salvation for us – if only we will listen and obey! In this case, the boy was touched in his heart into obedience after he 'came to his senses' and recalled scripture that says 'those whom I love I rebuke and discipline. So be earnest and repent.' – Revelation 3:19. He was moved by the Holy Spirit to repent and obediently turn from his wicked ways when the enormity of his chastisement hit him. 'I will return to my father's house' he said, as he stared hungrily at the disgusting pods the pigs were eating. Friend, let us not despise the painful chastising of the Lord, for God disciplines His loved ones and cares that all of us will be saved. Hebrews 12:6 says 'because the Lord disciplines the one He loves, and He chastens everyone He accepts as His son.' God as always, keeps His side of a bargain. His part of the forgiveness transaction was in fluid motion as usual. He had willingly opened His arms to enfold him, by causing the boy to consider obedience that leads into forgiveness and reconciliation. As we see it then, in the process of coming to his senses, the boy had been plugged into obedience, and he chose to say yes. Then also, the vigil the father in our parable kept on his roof-top was not in vain, for

God had further caused him to extend forgiveness long before his son's arrival, and the father had been obedient to this call by releasing the pain of the debt from his heart. When God prompts us to obey, we must jump at the opportunity. The angels are standing ready to begin the feast of reconciliation. Obedience to God is an expression of our love for Him. Obedience brings freedom to forgive. It is our obedience that gives us the opportunity to say thank you to God for forgiving us. Receiving forgiveness and extending it always strengthens our relationship with God in many ways. God is all about relationships. A relationship where we perceive Him as the loving father that He is. A relationship where we reverence His sovereignty and remember that He is in full control and He will never leave us nor forsake us as He says in Hebrews 13:5. A relationship of trust. 'If you love me, keep my commandments,' scripture says in 1John 5:2-3 and John 14:15. God enables us to obey Him in forgiveness because once we believe Christ and are saved, we are re-formed and we live for Christ and not for self. It takes courage to be obedient in forgiveness, but it is possible because of the events on the cross.

Looking back at our story, this prodigal son may have thought fleetingly of the shame he was bound to face from his older brother, and his household and most of all from his father. At that point, the draw to be obedient was not the physical hunger he felt, nor the ego that had pushed him to sin against his father in the first place. His eyes were drawn on Jesus, the blood spoke on his behalf and he obediently set off to make amends with his father. As mentioned above, God was also working on the father at the same time. Said father deliberately overlooked the hurt and pain his son caused him. He may have analyzed the depth of aversion his son had for him, but in obedience to God, he chose to forgive. What was his obedience based on? Scripture commanded that he forgive and he must have remembered how God had forgiven him his own many sins, and with the cross ever before him, he took the courageous step of obedience. Matthew 6:14 says 'For if you forgive other people when they sin against you, your Heavenly Father will also forgive you.' This father discerned that it was in his own best interest to forgive his younger son and to do so quickly. He did so to restore his relationship with God and then with son. It brought life back into his household where there was celebration and an air of freedom in his heart and his home. This is why he also encouraged his angry older son to revel in the joys of forgiveness. Luke 15:31 says 'My son,' the father said, 'you are always with me, and everything I have is yours.'

When we apply God's obedience in the realm of forgiveness, reconciliation comes quickly. In the same way, we all may face difficulty in seeking forgiveness from a person we may have offended or extending forgiveness to an offender. Our natural inclination does not go with obedience to the cross when one has sinned terribly or has been badly hurt. We tend to live on the level of our feelings, allowing them to control our lives. This makes our outlook on life distorted and poisonous, we contemplate filling our stomachs with pods meant for pigs – Luke 15:16. We would rather wallow in our depravation than seek God where we can find forgiveness through our obedience. It is imperative that we always listen out for God and come to our senses. We must be of the mind that forgiveness is a choice to obey the commands of scripture. Obedience allows us to live a life of joy and liberty. It is amazing how God can turn the most hardened heart around when we yield to Him in obedience. Human power cannot forgive our offender just like that. It is that act of obedience that makes us able to push towards forgiveness always. Romans 12:17-20 encourages us not to repay anyone with evil, but to do our possible best to live in peace with each other. When we obediently leave the sin with God, the needed coals are heaped on the head of our sinner without us having to lift a finger, Proverbs 25:22. We win back a friend when we desist from paying back sin. Jesus Christ was completely obedient to His Father, so that we could be saved, and He asks that we imitate His style of forgiveness so we inherit all that He has to offer. In the garden of Gethsemane, Jesus pleaded with His father to take the cup of suffering away, but He went on to say, not His will but the will of God, Luke 22:42. Had Jesus not pursued obedience, and taken the cross to Calvary, we would all be lost. Again, in Matthew 5:38-42, Jesus explains to us that we no longer need to justify the reasons for getting revenge, but to love our enemies as we obey God. We let God handle the crimes committed against us.

Forgiveness is what bridges the gap and makes every relationship possible. Forgiveness is truly the glue that keeps peace in place. Where there is fellowship there is peace, and that allows us to worship our Lord in spirit and in truth. A good relationship with God is good for the soul and such a relationship comes about through our obedience. Why do we keep pushing God aside, breaking that bond and wandering away to a distant country to squander our inheritance as the prodigal son did? How can we profess to love the Lord, and not respect His precepts? Nor trust Him. God requires nothing less of us than obedience. How best can we be obedient but by seeking and doing His will? Scripture says 'for all have sinned and fallen short of the glory of God – Romans 3:23,' but 'if we confess our sins, He is faithful and just to forgive us and cleanse us.' – 1John 1:9 We cannot have that beautiful relationship with God without adhering to that transaction of forgiveness in obedience. It is beneficial to us because an unforgiving spirit complicates and challenges our walk with Christ. We must know and accept immediately that it is forgiveness that spares us from the consequences of sin! In fact, God demands complete obedience, without delay always. Obedience presupposes that we love and trust Him and as we seek Him this way, He makes the tasks ahead of us easy. The beauty of being obedient in the face of the prospect to forgive is that God responds to such with peace. God responds by making our faith in Him stronger and allowing us to live a courageous and settled life. We must never undervalue the impact obedience will have when we keep our side of the forgiveness transaction. Obedience is a tool God uses to teach us how to rise above the wiles of the evil one. We all like sheep have gone astray says Isaiah 53:6, but if we obediently forgive, we too will be forgiven. It is a good thing to come to our senses, and make that decision to obediently restore our relationships by way of forgiveness.

III. Forgiveness: A lesson in Trust
'Trust in the Lord with all your heart, and lean not on your own understanding; in all thy ways acknowledge Him and he shall direct thy paths.'
-Proverbs 3:4-5

Trust in the Lord with all your heart, the Bible says. Once God sets the forgiveness ball rolling in our heart, we must trust the process, humbly accept His forgiveness so that we can forgive and be forgiven. In our parable under study, trust is a lesson that we come across and hopefully draw some lessons from.

The father trusted God, thereby was able to forgive his prodigal son completely. He longed for a renewed relationship with his son, because he trusted God to heal his heart of the anguish he had endured. This father also trusted God to forgive him for his own sins. Up there on the roof-top, as he gazed into the horizon, longing for his son's return, he most likely was in deep prayer, beseeching God to take away his sins and any sin that his household may have committed. It is possible that his trust level went up just because of the ordeal he sustained with his son. Prodigal son was also receiving his own lessons in trust. Luke 15:17-18 says 'When he came to His senses, he said, how many of my father's hired servants have food to spare, and here I am starving to death! I will set out and go back to my father and say to him.' He came to the realization that his reckless and irresponsible behavior had caused a deep rift between himself, God and his father. He had shattered the trust bond. Our loving Father, who is the originator of the forgiveness transaction quickens our hearts into contrition. In our brokenness, we repent and confess our sins, then God, who is ever ready, immediately jumps into action, enfolding us completely. This trust process allowed the younger son to regain confidence. He set out back to his father, knowing that God had forgiven him.

We are in the same predicament as the son in our story. We need forgiveness from our Father in Heaven as well as from the people we have hurt. We need to learn to forgive as well. We are desperate and unable to make headway in our lives when we harbor an unforgiving heart, or have not repented of a sin. The parable says in Luke 15:16 that 'He longed to fill his stomach with the pods that the pigs were eating, but no one gave him anything.' We long for our situation to change again, but no one will listen to us nor help us. We are so brokenhearted over our victim and the sin. We do not even believe that such a time is good enough to think about trust. No one can understand the depth of our pain. We might as well wither and die in our own sin. Nobody cares and how can God care too. These are common dispositions when we are deeply hurt, but here is when we have to rise and pick ourselves up. It is time to come to the Lord with a contrite and broken heart and trust that He will forgive us. Maybe, the incident against us will remind us of our own unforgiven sins – the many things we did to hurt our Lord and savior too. God is ready for us. The father in the story was ready for his son. He did not need a prepared speech. He understood just where he had to pick up and embrace his boy. The older son in this parable had no such qualms. He trusted only in himself, his friends and his duty towards hard work. He engaged his mind only on things that benefited him. His grievances held him captive because he did not trust God. He 'slaved away for years,' Luke 15:29 but nothing ever changed in his life because he was not prepared to let go his ego and give his all to God.

Friend, the grievances we have with each another should not stop us from trusting God first and then one another. This trust relationship should not remain an aspiration. We must resolve to trust God with everything. The need to forgive always suggests an infraction against us for which two options become available. Either we dwell on the sinner and their sins and allow the pain to fester or resolve to trust God, go to Him in prayer and request that He take away the pain of sin so we can reconcile with the sinner. Trusting God and praying that He help us in our quest for forgiveness is the best way to endure the process, and is a sure sign that the forgiveness transaction is blossoming. Well, 'what if our offender is a stranger?' You may ask. How then do we build trust, and why would we want to do so anyway? This is when we double up trusting God to heal us and praying for our offender too. As we trust God to see us through the process, He in His wisdom and power restores a stillness in our hearts and helps us rebuild our brokenness. Note that restoration may not necessarily be physical, but will be an internal letting go that brings peace of mind. Trusting sure brings Heavenly rewards. Such is the mystery and power of trust in forgiveness. Colossians 3:12 says to 'Bear with each other and forgive one another if any of you has a grievance against someone. Forgive as the Lord forgave you.' God does a much better job than we do in every situation. Trust Him.

IV. Perils of an unforgiving heart
'And his master was angry, and delivered him to the tormentors
until he should pay him all that was due to him.'
Matthew 18:34

Unforgiveness is when we impudently hang on to grudges or hurts in the face of God's good mercy towards us. In such a state, we tend to unwittingly push Jesus away while holding on to our grudges. I dare to call this act of unforgiveness brazen because it is a deliberate emotion that masquerades as excessive pain or hurt, sadness or anger at sins against us. We then tend to justify the reason for which we harbor an unforgiving heart. 'After all,' the devil whispers in our heart, 'the pain was excessive wasn't it?' or 'she really messed up your life, didn't she?' or 'He deserves to die for what he did, doesn't he?' As we lap up these exaggerated half-truths, we hide behind them and firmly withhold forgiveness. Yet by so doing, we say to God that the offenses against us are greater than those offenses we made against Him. We are exalting ourselves over Christ by magnifying our own sufferings and disparaging the work of the cross. Such an outlook yields many perils. Matthew 18:34 tells us that unless you forgive, you will be tormented. Unforgiveness causes us to be handed over to our tormentors. Have you ever wondered why you feel tormented and unable to rise up from your miseries? Scripture tells us that if we hold on to unforgiveness, we will be handed over to our tormentors. Thus, if we want to lead a torment free life, we forgive absolutely. When we learn to forgive, there is that sense of relief that comes upon us. Forgiveness feels like a new-found friend in our lives. We are tentative about it, and curious and unsure, yet willing to see how far we can go with this feeling. Jesus taught us that if we do not cultivate the power to forgive, God cannot forgive us also. This is what the forgiveness transaction is all about. The drive to forgive must be established in our hearts for this reason: You will be handed over to your tormentors if you do not forgive, says Matthew 18:35. Simply put, we are unable to dwell in God's presence if we harbor unforgiveness in our hearts. Bible says in James 2:13, 'judgment without mercy will be shown to anyone who has not been merciful. Mercy triumphs over judgment.'

Friend, I urge you to think about this: unforgiveness disproves our claim to salvation! Yes, indeed it does! Forgiveness is part of Heaven's currency. Christ has exchanged our sin for His grace; all at a very great cost to Himself. He has provided the forgiveness we all need in order to be saved. Bible says God gave His only begotten son, that whosoever believes in Him will be saved – John 3:16. If we believe that our sins were nailed to the cross with Jesus, if we believe that we can rise to accept forgiveness from Him because He longs that all will repent and receive that grace which is freely available to all, then we must get rid of all unforgiveness in our hearts. However, we do not all hear this salvation message because the 'pain' and 'anger' from the sin done us stands in the way. It is a major barrier to our salvation and hinders us from building a relationship of love and gratitude to God. Unless we forgive those who sin against us, will not God act against us? The action should be clear: if we have received mercy, we must dispense mercy for Christ's sake. Our claim to salvation will then endure.

We can refer to our parable for a good example of perils of an unforgiving heart. Both sons were in danger of being thrown to their tormentors for unforgiving hearts. The prodigal was flippant and disobedient, squandering his ill-gotten wealth in a distant country. The older son was egoistic, proud and had a cold heart. The younger was arrested by the Holy Spirit and came to himself in repentance. The older was self-absorbed, refusing to celebrate forgiveness with his father and brother. This father on the other hand embodies all who are aware of the dangers of unforgiveness and a hardened heart and move far away from such. He definitely must have been appalled at his younger son's sudden request for his share of the inheritance, and outraged by his older son's open display of hostility. It surely hit him hard to realize that he had borne two provoking and unappreciative boys who flaunted his good nature back at him in an unworthy manner. The father makes the verse in Ephesians 4:26-27 come to life ''Be angry, and do not sin: do not let the sun go down on your wrath, nor give place to the devil' When we do not forgive, the devil gets a foothold on us and does everything in his power to make our lives miserable. God's protective walls around us are removed when we refuse to be forgiving and we give an opening for the devil to derail us. This is what the father in our story avoided, and for all intents and purposes, his life was blessed. The unscrupulous attitudes of his sons stood as a stark reminder to him every day of the covenant relationship he had with God. It reminded him of how far God had brought him, and it kept him on his knees, praying a fervent prayer of thanksgiving as well as prayers for both his sons. This father was aware that unforgiveness always deprives us of grace, because it feeds the root of bitterness from which it originates.

The younger son in our story may also have felt the jolt of some of the perils that unforgiveness yields. He experienced the harsh results of a heart of stone which he had carried against his father and his older brother for years, and this feeling caused him to pay a terrible penalty in the end. In Luke 15:14 the Bible says 'After he had spent everything, there was a severe famine in that whole country, and he began to be in need.' His older brother certainly did not feel the same way, revealing to us that if we allow unforgiveness to remain in our hearts unchecked, the perils are dangerous. Let us contrast these two sons for a second, point out their differences and see what we can learn from both. First of all, here is a young precarious, self-loving younger lad, who came into money unscrupulously, stepping over everyone to do so. After wild living, the conditions abruptly change. This rich flippant boy is suddenly in great need. The rancor within him that he had carried around for so long was bearing fruit. He was in great torment, he was stressed, he lived in fear and he hated his surroundings and his job. His older brother too was on the verge of being thrown to his tormentors without even knowing it! He spoke with disdain and anger to his father, oblivious of the fact that he was no better than his lost brother. The rancor within him that he had carried around for so long was also bearing fruit. He had an angry outburst with his father, and refused to celebrate his brother's return. The difference between the two boys is that, the younger heeded the promptings of the Holy Spirit, came to his senses, and was delivered. The older, dwelling solely on his ego, could not hear the Holy Spirit's nudging and did not rise to receive forgiveness. The perils of unforgiveness are unswerving.

Which son are we? How different is it for us? With grudges the size of footballs shoved down our throats, dare we question God when we cannot rise up from troubles? Unforgiveness is unrepentant sin and is at odds with God's forgiving nature. Unforgiveness is perilous because it trivializes the suffering of Jesus Christ on the cross, and the entire salvation story. Maybe, the dangers of adopting an unforgiving heart has not sunk in yet? Such a heart inadvertently boasts self-promotion and breeds destructive emotions. Such a heart begets lonely isolation as the sons in our story portrays. Such a heart cannot be a part of the pact we have with God in the forgiveness transaction. When we host unforgiveness, we tend to have difficulty dealing with the wrong done us. We just think about the wounds and re-live the pain over and over in our hearts instead of releasing it to master Jesus. By so doing, the pain takes root in our hearts and minds, much to the delight of the devil, and this is where bitterness perpetuates in us. Slowly, this negative response will affect other areas of our life, such as our relationships, attitudes, and physical health. Interestingly unforgiveness is catalogued in medical books as a disease. Harboring negative emotions like anger and hatred creates a state of chronic anxiety, which does not help in the recovery process. An unforgiving heart produces feelings of discouragement that will eventually rob us of inner peace. We may look well and happy to the world, but within us, Christ's joy and peace are absent. Eventually despair sets in. The inner turmoil may become so great that we might desperately resort to worldly excesses such as drugs or alcohol in an effort to find relief. The younger son in our parable almost got to this point when pigs food begun to look like the only option. Satan hides behind the sin of unforgiveness to pull us down, always. We tell God we are sorry for all our sins every day, but then we bear grudges, thinking it righteously separate from our sins. Yet all sin is sin. Our reservation to Heaven is not secure if we do not forgive as God forgave us because we diligently separate this 'grudge sin' from other sins. An unforgiving heart is where the enemy is able to hide our sins from us. He hides behind that deadly sin, making us believe that because we were incredibly hurt, it is okay to hang on to it.

Friend, let us not belittle God's magnificent gift of love by disobediently harboring an unforgiving heart. Remember that holding a grudge against a sinner can cause us to fall from God's grace. What worse peril can there be than this? Scripture says in Romans 12:19, 'Dearly beloved, avenge not yourselves, but rather give place unto wrath: for it is written, Vengeance is mine: I will repay, says the Lord.' It is about time we muster the courage of leaving our pain from an infraction in God's hands. He knows how to deal with every situation impeccably. Believe that He will do a much better job at justice that we ever can. Let us not fail to forgive our offenders, nor harden our hearts no matter what nor hold that grudge at any cost. We will keep our cool in any hurtful situation, seek the Lord always, and even more so when we have to deal with forgiveness. For if we do not forgive, we run the risk of being thrown to our tormentors – Matthew 18:34, where it is impossible to pay our debt. We do not want to be there.

CHAPTER THREE
WHAT FORGIVENESS
IS NOT

We have considered at length the nature of forgiveness and the power behind its drive. Yet, powerful as it is, forgiveness is not a magic wand that immediately calms all conditions and soothes every traumatic experience when waved. It is God's gracious tool that He initiated to claim back relationships and heal injuries. However, some may hide behind 'forgiveness' to cover a multitude of destructive emotions, and contort its real functions. It is urgent therefore, that daily as we experience forgiveness, we focus on the fundamental purpose and effects so that we do not detract from its power nor take it for granted. After all, forgiveness is a learning curve, a testing of our hearts, to encourage us to love God, and teach us the true meaning of restored relationships. The devil is however hard on our heels to misguide us on anything that offer us peace and joy and brings us close to God. It is the evil one's sole interest to build a colony of unforgiving hearts, and a cunning way for him to stop us at all costs is by attacking this beautiful God-given concept called forgiveness. He tries continuously to confuse its meaning and function so we cease to practice it. This is why we have to identify the basic misconceptions so we do not falter on our journey through forgiveness.

One notorious trick the devil may use in his desire to dissipate the power of forgiveness is to cause us to believe that by forgiving, we are excusing or condoning sins against us. Absolutely not! We forgive out of humility and obedience to God, and free our own selves from the burden of injuries. So, as we release the hurt quickly from our hearts, we are not moved nor confused by any thought of minimizing what happened. It is a ploy to keep us imprisoned. We remember however, that the role we play as forgivers is necessary because although forgiveness is not the same as reconciliation, it is a definite pathway to restore a relationship. What more, when an offender does not or cannot repent, the work of forgiveness must fiercely persist for the same reasons stated above. There must be no fear in granting or requesting forgiveness by waiting for an apology or excusing it. The longer we wait, the more we tend to harbor resentment which eventually opens us up to more dangerous situations, much to the pleasure of the devil. Additionally, we cannot enforce justice by withholding forgiveness. We must determine in our hearts to let God be the avenger, because as it says in the bible, 'It is mine to avenge; I will repay, says the Lord.' - Romans 12:19b. We should not listen to the schemes of the devil who tries to convince us that we can fittingly dispense justice against our offender. It is best dear friend, to leave matters of justice to our just and loving God, who sees the heart of all men. Let us now observe some of the things forgiveness cannot accomplish so we can better understand the workings of the forgiveness transaction.

I. Forgiveness is not indulging sin

'For this son of mine was dead and is alive again; he was lost and is found. So, they began to celebrate.'
- Luke 15:24

To indulge sin is to close our hearts' eye to infractions against us and pretend it did not happen the way it did or it did not matter. A variety of reasons exist for indulging or condoning sin. Being criticized, fear of negative attention and fear that we will not be 'loved' anymore are some of the reasons for limiting the gravity of offenses. In our parable story, the father did not in any way condone his son's sinful behavior. When he said 'this son of mine was dead, but now is alive,' we realize that he was fully aware of the magnitude of the prodigal son's sins, but he was overcome by compassion and love and the need to forgive as Christ forgives. Here was a happy father who had run the forgiveness race and won the reconciliation prize. He understood that true forgiveness never excuses the infraction in any form so with the cross of Jesus ever before him, went through the granting of forgiveness in the correct way. We too must critically decipher between forgiving and condoning of sin so that we always choose to do the right thing when faced with the need to forgive. Some may think that by extending forgiveness, they are in other ways encouraging the sinner to repeat the act. In the same manner, some believe that the offender's contrition is permanently shelved when they are quickly forgiven for a sin. Far from the truth. By setting off back to the safety of his father's arms, this prodigal showed that his remorse was real. The father, being well aware of the sins of his sons, did not downplay the seriousness of his younger son's sin, nor did he hold the sins of his older son over his head. These were not times to distort or compromise his own moral standard. He described his lost son's sin as death itself. Dead to the law, dead in his sins, deprived of all spiritual life, God's enemy and lost. This is how his father saw him – as one facing the consequences of God's judgement; for all sin is actually against God. The father did not suppress his feelings in any way. By calling a spade a spade, and not indulging the sin, we are agreeing to transfer the sin from our system of justice to God's. The debt of the sin is then transferred from our ledger of accounts to God's, leaving all recompense to Him. The father also described his wayward son as lost. Younger son had lost all virtue and honor and there was no joy in his heart. With his penitent return to his father, God's grace took over. With the older son, Bible says, 'My son,' the father said, 'you are always with me, and everything I have is yours.' – Luke 15:32. Father did not indulge this fury that emanated from his older son when he refused to be awakened from his unforgiving heart, nor did father cower in the face of the deep animosity that spewed forth. He simply spoke the truth, and hoped that his words would lead to reconciliation for both his sons.

When we condone sin, we cannot successfully forgive. Our motive then is not forgiveness. It is never a good thing to make any allowances for sins against us or against God. Sin cannot be an excuse for anything. By overlooking what happened we indulge evil, and to put it bluntly, we become part of the problem. When we choose to forgive, we release a person from his indebtedness to us. We relinquish the right to seek personal revenge. Forgiveness therefore shows us that we are well aware that a wrong has been done against us, but we choose to recognize God's abundant grace over us in our own sinfulness. If we find ourselves diminishing a sin, and shoving it into the recesses of our minds and hearts, we must remember that we have not forgiven. We have just created a small space within us where we subconsciously store our hurts, and like a cancer, it maligns within us, festers and grows. That active release that must take place has not happened and the raw emotions that are associated with the sin have not been expressed and certainly not forgiven. Colossians 3:13 says 'bear with each other and forgive one another if any of you has a grievance against someone. Forgive as the Lord forgave you.' It is our Christian duty to forgive as we have been forgiven by God. God wants us to relinquish the right to personal revenge and live in harmony. The right way to do this is not to downgrade the act and swallow the hurt and disdain. Know exactly what happened and release it all to God. We have to let the work of the cross continue to matter in our hearts – a key element of the forgiveness transaction. Then we will be well on our way to possible reconciliation. In the meantime, forgiveness does not suggest that consequences of an action will not occur. Hebrews 12:6 says 'the Lord disciplines the one he loves, and he chastens everyone he accepts as his son.' Sin always needs atonement. It cannot be forgiven without a sacrifice which is what our Lord Jesus Christ endured for us.

II. Forgiveness is not reconciliation
'If your brother or sister sins against you, rebuke them, and if they repent, forgive them.'
- Luke 17:3

Forgiveness is the very beginning of rebuilding and strengthening a damaged relationship. It is not an end in itself but a fundamental and decisive step towards reconciliation. Though both are very necessary steps in the forgiveness transaction, forgiveness and reconciliation are not synonymous. One of the main stumbling blocks of unforgiveness is the notion that forgiveness must inevitably conclude in reconciliation. That does not have to be the case mainly because forgiveness is essentially a spiritual act whereas reconciliation is a physical undertaking. Moreover, we are not doing our offender a favor when we forgive them because the benefits of forgiveness are all ours. Forgiveness is done within our hearts, an inside job as some may put it, before it spills to the outside. Reconciliation is not necessarily the goal of forgiveness either because reconciliation requires mutual effort to restore trust. Both parties must be willing to restore the relationship. Reconciliation always assumes that there was a disruption or a break in the relationship, but due to a change of heart, that state of animosity and division has ended and there is now harmony and fellowship.

It is a Christian's duty to push towards reconciliation but this may not always happen at the point of forgiveness. Matthew 5:21-25 stresses that if there is unresolved disagreement with a person, we ought to work on this as soon as possible. We see this same urgency in Matthew 12:7 where Jesus tells us that the restoration of relationships is a very important practice. The verse above, Luke 17:3 also suggests to us that reconciliation and forgiveness are two related but separate processes. When we consider Jesus' words in Matthew 18:15, King James Version of the bible says 'Moreover if thy brother shall trespass against thee, go and tell him his fault between thee and him alone: if he shall hear thee, thou hast gained a brother.' We notice here, the insistence Christ places on the need to attempt resolving infractions amicably, in order to 'gain a brother.' God is truly keen on relationships, and the only way to get a good one going is to attempt reconciliations. Remember that reconciliation is the ultimate goal of restoring broken relationships, and though not always the case, the effort to do so must never cease. If our brother sins against us, we are admonished to rebuke him. We are urged to find a way to get close and talk about the sin. That is reconciliation in the making. The same verse says — and if they repent, forgive them. Good doses of prayer and fasting will enable us to move into the realm of reconciliation from forgiveness. The whole message of reconciliation is therefore centered around the love of God through the death of Christ. It is God's principal objective, that we be reconciled to Him and to each other.

This is the picture of the cross of Christ that we look at. Whereas forgiveness involves a mindset change in how we regard our offender, reconciliation involves a behavioral change between us and our offender. Forgiveness has been described as a gift to self while reconciliation is a gift to the offender.

A quick look at our parable story thoroughly explains the differences between forgiveness and reconciliation. While the prodigal son hurried towards forgiveness, his father also hastened towards reconciliation. Son was contemplating being forgiven by his father, yet father, who had longed for this day was way ahead. He had forgiven already and was eager to reconcile fully. Luke 15:22-23 says 'But the father said to his servants, Quick! Bring the best robe and put it on him. Put a ring on his finger and sandals on his feet. Bring the fattened calf and kill it. Let's celebrate.' Now what is wrong with this picture in Luke 15:22, you may ask? Sinners certainly should not be getting royal treatment, should they? Surely, this father here must have a scowl on his face, and a summons in his hands for the arrest of his younger son? His rapid advance towards his son should definitely be an effort to capture him and not to embrace? Yet it was all about reconciliation for the father. Jesus often preached on the need to be reconciled with each other. In Matthew 5:23-24, we learn that 'if you are offering your gift at the altar and there remember that your brother or sister has something against you, leave your gift there in front of the altar. First go and be reconciled to them; then come and offer your gift.' Jesus shows the importance of reconciliation in this passage. Much as we want to be right by God, the relationship is marred if our neighbor holds something against us. It will be difficult for God to receive our gift offerings if our hearts are not free of grudges. We should yearn to reconcile with our Father in Heaven and extend that special relationship to our offenders. Reconciliation is therefore as important as forgiveness.

Remember that forgiveness aims at reconciliation but as stated earlier it is certainly not the same. The father in our parable went to great lengths to express his kindness to his son. He was moved by compassion, another attribute of God's love, and of the forgiveness transaction. He noticed nothing but the person that he loved. He had successfully separated the crime from his son and showed him love. Forgiveness does not aspire to seek vengeance for trespasses and neither does reconciliation. From the father's action in our parable story, the scripture from Ephesians 4:32 becomes real. 'Be kind and compassionate to one another, forgiving each other just as in Christ God forgave you.' Celebration was foremost on this father's mind, as our verse above indicates. He had waited a long time for this reconciliation to take place. Forgiveness however, had taken place prior to that. Do not for a second think that him doing his son's bidding or forgiving or reconciling with his son were signs of weakness. No, this father was a strong man. Strong because he resolved in his heart to go God's way. He knew the love of God and was aware of the many times God's forgiveness had swept over him. He identified with the scripture where Christ said 'Father forgive them for they don't know what they do.' – Luke 23:34 He knew that his son had been badly wounded by a case of unforgiveness and needed that show of love that accompanied forgiveness, so that this son could heal properly. As such, much as we yearn to reconcile with our offenders, we always remember that reconciliation cannot occur without forgiveness. Not vice versa though, since we can forgive at all times, because it is the conduit to reconciliation.

What is the take away? That forgiveness is great, but taking a step further into reconciliation is also great. Jesus while on the cross said to the thief in Luke 23:43, 'today, you will be with me in paradise.' The sinner, in faith had repented and believed in a forgiving father. God's abundant grace worked overtime in his heart. He called out unto the Lord, and Christ not only forgave, but granted immediate reconciliation. Though we are not at liberty to reconcile with an unrepentant soul, we must, for the sake of our own forgiveness, release the offender from their sin and stand ready to be reconciled. It is a calling that we all have and must exercise through the power of the Holy Spirit. We must always be motivated by the grace of God, the forgiveness of our own sins and gratitude to be transformed, to push on towards reconciliation. For the Bible says 'Let us not grow weary in doing good for in due season we shall reap, if we do not lose heart.' – Galatians 6:9 We are called to be ambassadors of reconciliation, to be courageous, humble and vulnerable, moving the extra mile to remove the enmity of this world to the cross of Jesus who did the costly work for peace to reign. God wants to reconcile with us at all costs. How will this love story end? Will we rise to the occasion literally? Will we keep the pact of the forgiveness transaction in motion? Will we seek forgiveness and pass it on? Get on with it then.

III. Forgiveness Is not Forgetting
'For this son of mine was dead and is alive again; he was lost and is found. So they began to celebrate.'
- Luke 15:24

Do not think for a moment that the father in our parable 'forgot' the incident that sent his younger son departing to a distant country. He was very much aware of every painful detail. He had prayed about the raw emotions it elicited while he was seeking his own forgiveness and that of his household. He remembered every aching aspect of how broken he felt when his younger son deserted him. Yet, he forgave him and longed to see his son again to be reconciled with him. This father was also well aware of the blatant arrogance of his older son and the many times this son looked down on him and rubbed the events leading to his younger brother's departure in his face, portraying him as a weak father. These, from a worldly perspective, were very sore points for him, but thank God for grace. It was undeniable that his boys had been a great source of pain, but he continued to spend a lot of time in prayer for them. He was grateful to God that he had nothing but love in his heart for those two. So, would you say he forgot his sons' sinful events against him?

Contrary to popular belief, the adage to 'forgive and forget,' is not found in the Bible. It has become a very popular saying all over the world, and many may think that if we are unsuccessful in removing details of an offense from our hearts, then we are failures in our quest to offer forgiveness or seek God's forgiveness. However, to 'forgive and forget' is largely unrealistic. How does one forget an incident from which one suffered – in some cases permanent consequences? Let us clarify this notion immediately. Forgiveness does not necessarily constitute forgetting what happened. It will be improbable to remove the thought of an awful incident from our minds in our desire to forgive. For example, if an offender inflicts a wound on us that leaves a physical scar on a prominent part of our body, it would be impossible to forget the incident. In the same vein, it seems like an unrealistic feat to forget our relative's killer, the rapist, the 'friend' who betrayed us and many, many more. Some genuinely want to forgive offenses but are unable to do so successfully because they have bought into the forgive and forget theory. When they realize how overwhelming this tall order is, they give up completely! Why? They are unable to forget the incident, so they push the deed into the recesses of their hearts and it 'goes away' without any forgiveness rendered. It turns into a grudge, and they achieve nothing. They have neither forgiven nor forgotten because they were overcome by the entire process. It is time to debunk that adage, so that we can all actively forgive our offenders, whether we remember details of the infractions or not. Let's start with a short exercise: Why are our bodies almost always permanently scarred from large injuries but little scuffs mostly just fade away? Also, when we look at scars on our bodies, what do we think? Do we remember with gratitude that God spared our lives in a particular scar causing incident? Does it lead us to pray a thanksgiving prayer unto the Lord? Do the scars remind us of the part we may have played in self-harm? Do they help us make changes to our lives so we are not placed in a position where we get hurt again? Get my drift? If we stare blankly at our scars and are not moved in anyway, then there are no lessons to be drawn. In the same way, the hurt done against us, or us against God cannot be fully forgotten because there is work to be done with them! We must remember what happened in order to release them from our heart and place them at the feet of Jesus. The pain must invoke a feeling of gratitude and love, that turns us towards God. He will cause that heart of stone to melt towards our offender as well.

However, let us complicate matters with two representations where forgetting becomes important. Apostle Paul states in Philippians 3 to forget what is behind and strain towards what is ahead as we press on towards the goal to win the prize for which God has called us Heavenward in Christ Jesus. Here, Paul asks us to keenly forget past hindrances in our quest to get closer to God. Paul teaches us to make every effort to focus on the present and the future rather than live in the past; to refuse to allow past successes inflate pride or past failures to deflate our self-worth. This manner of active 'forgetting' protects us from our own egos and helps us to keep our eyes only on Christ in all our endeavors. Secondly, God chooses to remember our past sins no more – Hebrews 8:12 and also in Isaiah 43:25, God says when He forgives us, He remembers our sins no more. That is, He practices 'Forgive and Forget!' He forgets our sins! So why then can't we also totally forget the sins against us in our effort to forgive? Why can't we instantly forget the pain in order to make forgiving easier? Well, what we must realize is that, when God says He 'remembers our sins no more,' He has chosen in His sovereignty never to hold our sins against us when He forgives! He can literally forget our sins, because He has no use for them when they are expunged. He chooses not to hold any sin that He has previously purged from the sinner against them ever again. You and I on the other hand, can never expunge sins by the blood of Jesus as God does, so we cannot afford to forget sins like our God. The chance that we will never come around to forgiving our offender if we promptly forgot the sin is too high. This is why we must remember our offenders' sins so we can take them to the cross of Jesus.

In view of the above considerations, God will cause us to remember the offenses against us so we can pay full attention to releasing them from our hearts. Indeed, we may from time to time forget a grievance here and there, but the big wounds against us must be remembered in order to praise God for helping us survive our ordeals, then as we relish in gratitude, we use the same grace to enthusiastically offer forgiveness too. God allows us to remember the good, the bad and the ugly just so we can also remember that His grace is always sufficient for us. Psalm 103:2 says 'Praise the Lord, my soul and forget not all His benefits.' In that same spirit of remembering, we are charged not to forget those suffering for the sake of Christ, and those in prison – Hebrews 13:3, Paul also asks to be remembered as he endures his chains – Colossians 4:18. Thus remembering takes on a completely different mission than its usual sense! Remembering here enriches our prayer lives greatly. We remember the situation in order to move into the prayer realm, and also in order to effectively forgive! Moreover, we remember that our offenders have brought us to the brink of despair, and the best place to be when we are in our pig-pen is at the feet of Jesus, where we can rise up and become overcomers. We simply cannot forget because it is Christ who gives us the courage to soar into forgiveness. We no longer hold the offense against the sinner because of the blood of Jesus. We choose to remember our infractions without rancor, and set all offenses aside as we appropriate the future God promises to those who love Him. Ephesians 2:10. We are able to smile at all our other wonderful blessings that God bestows on us each day. We do not forget the sin, but we daily choose to live for God's glory and the more the incident comes to mind, the louder our praise will be.

IV. Forgiveness does not Neutralize Justice

'How much more severely do you think someone deserves to be punished who has trampled the Son of God underfoot, who has treated as an unholy thing the blood of the covenant that sanctified them, and who has insulted the Spirit of grace? For we know Him who said, it is mine to avenge; I will repay and

again, The Lord will judge His people. It is a dreadful thing to fall into the hands of the living God'
-Hebrews 10:29-31

It is a worthy learning point for every Christian to discern that God is the ultimate judge and we are not. It is also a very good thing to know that God can take care of all our vulnerabilities much better than we ever can. Human as we are, our first instinct is to strike back hard when we are hurt. We want our offenders to suffer as much as we have and more. We cannot bear it if he or she seems to walk away unpunished. We want justice and we will only consider forgiveness when we see justice. A justice that will satisfy our ego. A justice that will take the pain we endure away. Except the pain never seems to end because our idea of justice is so dissimilar to God's plan for justice. Remember that God already charged our sins to Christ's blood on the cross and offered us righteousness instead. We, just like our offenders, hurt Him badly when we sin, but His form of justice is atonement by His own blood. God is asking us to release the offender over to Him so that ultimate justice may be served. When we refuse to forgive, we are in our own way taking justice out of the hands of a just God and enacting our own wrath and anger upon our offender. But unbeknownst to us, it just might be that we were not created to bear this heavy burden. It is our human endeavor to prove that we love God always and once we have ascertained forgiveness from God, the onus is on us to give God the go ahead to take care of said justice - transferring the right to exact punishment or revenge for our offender to God. We forgive by mastering the separation of sin and sinner. Yes, what our offender did is beyond wrong, but ours is to learn how to separate the two, placing the sin on the cross and learning to love the sinner again. What a formidable task I hear you say, but that is our lot and it is possible because the events of the cross have already taken place. It is a grace that is bestowed upon us when we ask God for it. Forgiveness does not lessen the consequences of the action against us, nor does it neutralize justice. Justice comes to right a wrong and our God is well aware of that. In Jesus, we find both justice and forgiveness. He took the weight of our sin to the cross and died for us and at that time, justice was served. The Bible says 'for the wages of sin is death.' – Romans 6:23 By forgiving and seeking forgiveness we are released from that bondage prison and freed to live our lives in peace, but when we do not, the hurt and anger turn into bitterness which imprisons us and poisons our souls. Hence, we forgive regardless, knowing that death on the cross has justified the sin.

We may sometimes feel the need to be vengeful towards our offender, to help assuage the hurt they caused, but our human form of justice is reactive and never proactive like God's justice. We must therefore take courage and forgive our offenders with the faith and knowledge that our God of justice will act on our behalf, because the love Christ showed on the cross has done the work. When we are conscious of this fact we do not worry about personal justice again. It is true that natural consequences of sin may continue to manifest even after repentance. After all, if we destroy our bodies in sin, we should not always expect instant recovery. Likewise, if we squander all our wealth in an unworthy manner, like the prodigal son did, we know that we may have to start from the bottom step of the ladder. Rebuilding of trust and wealth will not be automatic just because we repented and are forgiven. On the contrary, because we are forgiven, we may still suffer – to keep us humble, but God promises never to leave nor forsake us. He will avenge our troubles. Rest assured and continue to pray as we allow the forgiveness process to wash over us.

This prodigal son in Luke 15, was aware that justice had to prevail for the forgiveness transaction to run its natural course. He obviously did not want to be a hired servant, but in his broken state, he knew that full restoration to son-ship would not be a surety. He was just grateful that humility had taken the place of his previous heart of stone. Thank God for His grace to pardon absolutely as He sees fit. Acts 3:19 says 'repent, then and turn to God, so that your sins may be wiped out, that times of refreshing may come from the Lord.' The father in our story did not take the matter into his own hands. He knew the capabilities of God so he interrupted his son's confession in Luke 15:22 'But the father said to his servants, Quick! Bring the best robe and put it on him. Put a ring on his finger and sandals on his feet.' As such, though forgiveness does not mean automatic restoration, our God has the power to do so. Let us then approach Him with true brokenness over our sins and see Him perform His finest for us. In like manner, let us forgive our offenders and stand ready to enfold them, leaving the consequences to our God. For though forgiveness may cost us personal justice, pride and our rights, consider that it cost Christ His life by Him meeting our greatest offenses with utmost grace. Friend, forgiveness does not diminish justice; it just entrusts it to God. He guarantees the right retribution always.

CHAPTER FOUR
WHAT FORGIVENESS
CAN ACCOMPLISH

Have you ever considered what forgiveness truly accomplishes? Other than obviously eliminating an unforgiving heart, forgiveness is able to do so much. Forgiveness is that great teacher of humble obedience. When embraced, it gives us a delicious taste of the mercy of God, and considerably lightens the load in our hearts. Forgiveness goes all out to eliminate fear because it heals the grudges that debilitates our souls. Forgiveness is that bridge upon which an aggrieved party can reconcile with his offender, allowing restoration to be within reach. It protects our emotions from negative outbursts, emboldening us to worship God fervently so that we can receive a new joy in our hearts. Whenever we lift our hearts up to God in repentance, Heaven rejoices. When we open our hearts in compassion to forgive, there is always a fresh spring in our step because our burdens are literally taken away. Forgiveness also allows us to recognize a peace that passes all understanding when God pours out His love on our brokenness. The best thing we can therefore do is to cultivate a forgiving heart so we can accomplish the many joys that God has in store for us.

I. An Act of Worship

'Praise the Lord, my soul, and forget not all His benefits,
who forgives all your sins and heals all your diseases.'
-Psalm 103:2-3

The miracle of forgiveness is an exclusive event that is perfectly exhibited in the private moments of worshipping God. When we lift our hearts unto the Lord in worship, mercy comes down. In worshipping this awesome Lord and magnifying Him, He sends down the strength and power needed to be compassionate. Whenever we enter into God's splendor and give Him honor, He hears our cries of brokenness and repentance and responds with all the love. Then as we forgive others and beseech God to take the sin away from our offenders, we begin to exalt the awesome Name of God. Forgiveness must always manifest itself in majestic worship. As the father in our parable from Luke 15 stood vigil on his roof-top alone, desiring his younger son's return, he must have prayed this prayer fervently 'Who is a God like you, who pardons sins and forgives the transgressions of the remnant of His inheritance? You do not stay angry forever but delight to show mercy. You will again have compassion on us; You will tread our sins underfoot and hurl all our iniquities into the depths of the seas.' – Micah 7:18-19 These words flooded his mind and he bowed down in worship, thinking about his own salvation and his longing to reunite with his son again. Our asking for and receiving of forgiveness must always trigger worshipping God. We tell God that the sin is against Him and Him alone. What happened to us is negligible when compared to what happened to Jesus. In our forgiveness therefore, we honor God and magnify the one who is able to take away sins and remember them no more. Remember the woman with the alabaster jar in Matthew 26:7? She worshipped Jesus with all she had. At the feet of Jesus, she showed how much she cherished Him by anointing His feet with expensive perfume. Worship causes God to forgive us quickly. As we worship, we tell Him that we are vulnerable and He is all powerful. We tell Him that we have no power to forgive ourselves or our offenders but He does – and how quick He is to forgive when He sees that! As Christ loves and welcomes sinners into His midst, we the forgiven sinners, also love and worship Him even more. This is what the forgiveness transaction accomplishes. God's amazing feat of forgiveness is offered as we worship Him, entrusting our all to Him. It is urgent therefore, that we allow God to saturate our minds as we direct all our thoughts to Him, especially when we feel defenseless by the sin caused against us, or our sins that we want Him to forgive. The vulnerability should make us move towards God always. As we release our offender's grudge into God's mighty hands, we acknowledge His sovereignty. For who is able to pardon but Him? Who is able to wipe away sins with His own blood but God. We lift His Name up and exalt Him for the work He does in us, as He teaches and perfects our faith. 'When you stand praying,' the Bible says in Mark 11:25, 'if you hold anything against anyone, forgive him, so that your Father in Heaven may forgive you your sins.' The forgiveness transaction necessitates a time of worship from our side of the pact. That spiritual phenomenon of forgiveness cannot be effected in a vacuum. Our minds have to choose to release our offender in spite of the heavy burden of sin that separates us. How on earth do we manage that if we do not invoke God's power? In the same vein, as we repent and confess our sins to God, prayer is necessary, and not just any prayer, but a prayer that sees God as holy and majestic, worthy to pardon and able to set us free. In the presence of God, as we release the grudges, the resentments and the aches, we believe that God is mighty and will pardon all the hurt. The blood of Jesus works overtime when cries of worship reach Heaven. Hebrews 9:12 describes how Jesus sought eternal redemption for us all with His very blood. That blood carries with it forgiveness itself. So, all grievances must be dealt with in relation to God. We relate to Him in forgiveness, we relate to Him in pain and we relate to Him in grudges. We lift Him up high and let His peace wash over us. When we are forgiven and we do not forgive, God is not worshipped. How do we say 'may Your Name be exalted, when deep in our hearts, we are held captive by the wrongs done us? Letting go of the pain and placing it into the hands of God magnifies Him. When someone hurts us badly, we must turn our eyes first on our Sovereign God and acknowledge Him alone as King of kings and Lord of lords who takes away the sins of man. Worshipping the Lord releases the sin into His care, by separating the sinner from His sin, so that God can bring spiritual relief to both.

If there is any time to draw closer to God in worship, it is during our most vulnerable moments when we feel dejected and broken. When the emotions are raw, and we are deeply hurt by a sin committed against us, and nothing seems to make sense. Then is the time to draw close to God and acknowledge His supremacy and His ability to judge the sin as is rightly deserving. Lift Him up in this matter. An act of worship is when we realize that the sin was against us but ceases to be about us. It is about God who is able to wipe it clean. When we place the trauma into His care in worship, He is highly honored. We trust in His all-knowing, all powerful ability, and we are bereft of the pain and anger. Nevertheless, if we think for a moment that we can pray to God with the view of having Him hurt our offender, then we need to ask God for forgiveness. Our prayers should never be an effort to use God to do our bidding. Our just God knows what is right and what is best for us as well as our offender. We must never endeavor to worship God to exact punishment on our offenders. No! 1Peter 3:9 says 'do not repay evil with evil or insult with insult. On the contrary, repay evil with blessing, because to this you were called so that you may inherit a blessing'. Romans 12:17-18, say the same thing and goes on to encourage us to live at peace with all, as far as it depends on us. Ours is an act of humble reverence, to acknowledge that God is omnipresent, omniscient and omnipotent in nature. This kind of genuine worship also allows us in the capacity of victim, to humble ourselves as we crown God judge of all.

The prodigal son in our parable learned the need to worship God. He reflected on his wasteful ways, and praised God for taking away the blinders from his heart's eye. When God gently touched his heart, the boy abruptly 'came to his senses!' He whispered to God, asking for forgiveness. He acknowledged God's majesty and worth. This act of worship allowed him to let go of his deep pride as the Holy Spirit empowered him to lift up the Name of God more and more. When he made his decision to go back home to his family, his eyes were on God. He said 'I have sinned against Heaven and against you,' – Luke 15:18 Right then, many firsts occurred in his life! He acknowledged God first! He examined his situation with God first then he repented of his sin to Him first, then as he begun to worship God, the work of the cross gained new meaning, humbling him completely before he turned to go back to his father. Worship empowers us to look to God first in times of crisis, then allows us to take the bold step back to our offender or the person we offended.

As we contemplate the forgiveness transaction, our prayer should be that Holy Spirit will help us raise our hearts in worship when we encounter hurtful situations. That we will always be reminded of how our God first forgave us, and how He is ready to forgive us every day as we worship Him. That, through our worship, He will lift us out of our drudgery so we can forgive our offenders with all our hearts. It is our forgiveness of others that becomes an act of worship, for as we worship in forgiveness, we humbly ask God to help us not to dwell on the sin, nor bring it up over and over, nor let it fester in our hearts nor hinder our personal relationships. May His Name always be glorified.

II. Deflating Pride
'The eyes of the arrogant will be humbled and human pride brought low; the Lord alone will be exalted that day.'
-Isaiah 2:11

Nothing clouds our reasoning more than pride because it gives us a very distorted look of ourselves and makes it hard for us to believe we may need forgiveness. Many words come to mind as we try to define pride. Condescending, conceit and vanity all describe the inward-looking emotion that inflates a person's own worth in society. Pride is deceptive because one always sees him or herself from their own point of view and never from God's standpoint, and since pride means a sense of superiority over others, he or she may be going down a path of depravity without realizing it. A depraved lifestyle is the fastest way into the tormentor's fire. Basically, when we exalt ourselves, instead of God, we are proud. Another simple way of understanding pride is to capitalize the 'I' in pr-I-de — meaning 'I' or self is of sole importance.

There are many Bible verses warning about pride, and the caution here is that pride is the source of all sins. It may surprise you to know that the first sins recorded in the Bible all had significant expressions of pride. Cosmic treason was what Lucifer committed against our sovereign God, when his pride got him to defy God and was subsequently driven from His presence - Ezekiel 28:11-19. In Proverbs 8:13 the Bible says 'I hate pride and arrogance, evil behavior and perverse speech.' Bible also says in Proverbs 16:5, 'The Lord detests all the proud of heart. Be sure of this: They will not go unpunished.' James 4:6 also reads, 'God opposes the proud but gives grace to the humble,' Interestingly, many of the verses on pride that we encounter in the Bible carry a notion of combat. We see a God who will go to war with pride and always win. God detests pride because it is the root of sin, and we all know how God feels about sin – He hates sin.

The forgiveness transaction is a two-way street. The offer and the receipt. God offered Jesus on the cross at Calvary to forgive all. It is up to us to receive this call of forgiveness. Once received, we also offer forgiveness to our offenders. If our hearts are hardened, there is no way we can forgive our offenders. Remember the verse that says 'forgive us our debts as we forgive our debtors?' – Matthew 6:12. Pride does not know how to receive or offer forgiveness. If it is not deflated somehow, one is in danger of missing Heaven all together. Yet, we are creatures of pride for a reason because if pride is not present, we cannot overcome it and humble ourselves unto the Lord. In other words, if we did not know pride and experience it, we would have difficulty appreciating the beauty and essence of humility when it comes upon us. It is incumbent that we choose to be humble every time to avoid God's punishment. Philippians 2:3 says 'do nothing out of selfish ambition or vain conceit. Rather, in humility value others above yourselves.' Pride cometh before a fall, the saying goes, for you cannot fall if you are already down. Another catastrophic trigger of pride is our ego. Whereas pride will flaunt its self-satisfaction, ego exposes her self-admiration all the way. So, pride is rooted in the heart and ego is born in the mind. Ego tends to interpret forgiveness and reconciliation as signs of weakness as though if we forgive, then what happened to us was deserved. Ego demands that we refuse forgiveness because it provides us with great power and control over our offender. I must quickly refute the notions of pride and ego that seem to suggest that forgiveness is a concession or an act of self-endangerment. Not at all! Forgiveness is a liberating gift from God that must be lavishly applied.

Let us examine our parable for a second. In Luke 15:12, the prodigal son starts out full of pride and arrogance. He has no respect for his father, nor does he care that his words may be very hurtful towards him. He demands his share of his inheritance with a sense of right. One would think that a person with such a heart of stone cannot be turned around. Yet with God, all things are possible. If a person has a heart of stone, and believes they cannot forgive their offender for sinning against them, nor be forgiven because of the enormity of their own sins, just watch what God can do. In verse 17 of Luke 15, the prodigal son 'came to his senses!' With nowhere to turn and his dwindled funds, he went into a time of dejected introspection. As he questioned his ego and assessed his deeds, he realized that none of his party friends came to his rescue and for the first time in his life he was truly alone. Pride indeed cometh before a fall.

Meanwhile, his older brother, believing himself to be the pious one, was also prideful. In Luke 15:28-29 we read that 'The older brother became angry and refused to go in. So his father went out and pleaded with him. But he answered his father, 'Look! All these years I've been slaving for you and never disobeyed your orders. Yet you never gave me even a young goat so I could celebrate with my friends.' He would not go and join in the celebration of his younger brother's return. The pride in him did not allow forgiveness because it would take the glory off him. In the heart and mind of the older brother, to forgive was to weaken the boundary between himself and his brother and that would discredit him, a prospect he dreaded. He could not let that happen. Pride kept him focused on the past, always reflecting on the sins of his brother. We learn from his attitude that pride preoccupies us with the past as a matter of self-preservation. We also learn that had the prodigal son not faced the difficulties of hardship, where he longed to fill his stomach with the detested pig pods, he probably would not have recognized humility. That is what it takes at times; having to surrender our all, in order to rise above. So, when this younger son came to his senses, he made a pact with God – that he would let go of his pride so he could take on a humble spirit from the Lord. He achieved this by first forgiving himself of his foolishness. Then as he cried out unto the Lord, God forgave him, and prepared him to meet his father.

Friend, we should not let pride get in our way, for its fall is hard and painful. Pride has no place in the forgiveness transaction. It perpetuates a negative situation by choosing not to forgive, and it is our decision not to forgive that invites the negativity because forgiveness is a release from negativity. Let us allow God to penetrate our hearts of stone, such that we will always come to our senses. Forgiveness can deflate pride, but we have to be ready to come to our senses. Satan works tirelessly in the area of pride. He reasons with our egos and our rights. 'You do deserve this glory' he appeals. The seemingly nonchalance of these personal appeals can be lost on us when we are not familiar with the forgiveness transaction. We must live our lives with the work of the cross ever before us. This work is about forgiveness wiping away our sins where Christ takes upon Himself all our pride and arrogance. The moment we take our eyes off the cross, we fall into the enemy's ruse, where self becomes more important than Christ. Indeed, forgiveness is a powerful arrow in a Christian's quiver that puts down the schemes of the evil one quickly. Refuse to buy into the devil's traps by embracing all manner of forgiveness. There is power in forgiveness.

III. Riches in Mercy
'But because of His great love for us, God, who is rich in mercy, made us alive with Christ even when we were dead in transgressions – it is by grace you have been saved.'
-Ephesians 2:4-5

Mercy simply means compassion or sympathy which the father in our parable demonstrates very well. As he hurtled down the dusty trail eager to embrace his approaching son, the words in the Ephesians 2 verses above reverberated in his heart and mind. How often this father had fallen on his knees to acknowledge the great love of God. Now with his own eyes, he could see his younger son coming back to receive forgiveness and be reconciled. 'This son of mine was dead in his transgressions,' he said, 'he was lost and is found. It is by grace, Oh Lord, it is by Your grace.' What a joy, and what relief when we stand at the brink of forgiveness and drink in deep. God looks on at us and feels love and tenderness towards us. He is the author of great love and mercy which is evident right from the works in the garden of Eden. There, God, standing ready to enfold, made garments for Adam and Eve in spite of their great sin. This mercy is seen throughout the Bible in a variety of ways. The parable of the good Samaritan in Luke 10:33 reveals the essence of mercy. With mercy came the practical demonstration of kindness that the Samaritan showed. In Psalm 136, we are assured of God's mercy that endures forever. Then mercy's crowning moments came when

Jesus called out 'it is finished' on the cross at Calvary. The forgiveness transaction was complete. That cycle of negativity was broken. Healing had been provided for the unforgiving heart. Relationships were repaired. Generosity of spirit had been created, fellowships revitalized. Joy was restored and God was glorified. His riches in mercy accomplished all of this on the cross at Calvary. He had provided full forgiveness for our sins by the blood that Jesus shed. Salvation had come. God's rich mercy towards us had caused Him to act on our behalf and take away our suffering on the cross.

What was the caveat of this gracious gift of mercy? Obediently reaching out in faith to receive the riches of forgiveness. Are we able to do that? Can we mimic the great love of God and revitalize a relationship previously broken due to sin? This was the father's goal all along in our parable. He had forgiven his son from day one, but now, he had the opportunity to reveal his forgiveness and show love. In like manner, the younger son had also experienced the riches of God's mercy. In spite of his hunger pangs and weak disposition, he pressed on towards his father in total surrender. He, a regenerate sinner now had the opportunity to become a reborn soul with a new life of sanctification. He had allowed God's great love to work on him, he had seen the horrible effects of pride, he had experienced rich mercy and even if he did not make it to son-ship, boy was he going to try! He was bereft of words to describe the joy he felt, having made up his mind to walk the street of forgiveness. 'Oh, what peace we often forfeit, oh what needless pain we bear, all because we do not carry, everything to God in prayer.' A version of Joseph Scriven's hymn7 was in his heart and with every painful step towards his father, the younger son felt more and more revitalized. Titus 3:5 says 'He saved us, not on the basis of deeds which we have done in righteousness, but according to His mercy,' and this mercy is '...new every morning for great is His faithfulness.' – Lamentations 3:23 It is imperative that we draw from this well as deeply as we can. We ought to allow God's forgiveness to wash over us always. Instead of seeing the guilt, the hurt and the pain, let us join the psalmist and count our blessings as is portrayed in Psalm 103. Our God has pardoned all our iniquities and crowned us with loving kindness and compassion. Take out the malice, strife and wickedness, and seize with reverence, God's rich mercy. Micah 7:18 says 'Who is a God like You, who pardons sin and forgives the transgression of the remnant of His inheritance? You do not stay angry forever but delight to show mercy.'

Dear Friend, those who know a merciful God should always love mercy. If we understood the depth of God's forgiveness, we would also always be ready to forgive because God's merciful heart aches over the grief our sins brought into the world. God's great love and rich mercy makes all things well so as we grow in His likeness, our hearts must also ache to release all resentments and grudges that we harbor against our offenders. Our spiritual life is revitalized when we live in union with Christ. We who were buried are raised up with Him. His work on the cross should never be in vain. If we carry in our hearts any unforgiven sin, we must take that bold step towards forgiveness by taking it to the Lord in prayer. Likewise, if we bear anyone a grudge for an offense committed against us, we take it to the Lord in prayer and forgive. For the Bible clearly states that if we do not forgive their sins, God will not forgive ours too – Matthew 6:14-15. As we meditate on His mercy and grow in His likeness, His rich mercy will be a meaningful part of our daily living and we can join the psalmist and sing with him in Psalm 23:6 'surely goodness and mercy will follow me and I will dwell in the house of the Lord forever.'

IV. Secure your reservation to Heaven
'He that cannot forgive others, breaks the bridge over which he himself must pass if he would ever reach, for everyone has need to be forgiven' - George Herbert8

The Kingdom of Heaven is likened to the parable Jesus told of the wicked servant, in Matthew 18, who was forgiven a large debt but immediately turned around, choking his fellow servant and demanding to be paid a puny amount owed to him. The question I often ask is how could this wicked servant have forgotten the greatest compassion that had been shown him in such a short time? Did he not have contrition in his heart when he fell to his knees begging his master for mercy? Do we find ourselves in such predicaments, begging and confessing without contrition? Pretending to be one thing, but not meaning it? Does Jesus' work on the cross mean nothing? Are we just trying to satisfy our ego and move on to please self? The story goes on to say his master, after finding out how wicked the servant was to his fellow servant handed him over to his tormentors until he paid back the debt he owed. Our Heavenly Father, the story concludes, will do same to us unless we forgive our brother from our hearts. Is your reservation to Heaven secure? Some are of the view that going to Heaven is automatic when they die. Others think knowing 'the story' of Jesus Christ is a sure way of going to Heaven. Some also cannot see past the God-side of the forgiveness transaction. The God-side of the forgiveness transaction shows a merciful God who has forgiven and stands ready to enfold always. Yet a careful study of Matthew 6:7-15 reveals that if we do not forgive, our Heavenly father will not forgive us. Yet still, others look at works or wealth to determine if they are Heaven bound. Much has been said about how to get into Heaven. We tend to pick and choose what works for us. The young ruler asked Jesus in Luke 18:18 'Good Teacher, what must I do to inherit eternal life?' What the ruler considered upright and worthy to secure his position in Heaven was so far from what Christ teaches. His ignorance made him believe to be full of Heavenly virtues. He was nonplussed when Jesus mentioned the one thing that he lacked – a relationship with God. We can have everything, own everything, obey all the commandments, but never have eternal life if we do not fulfil the law to love God with our all. This ruler was a good idolater, loving his works and his wealth more than God. 1Corinthians 6:9a says 'Or do you not know that wrongdoers will not inherit the kingdom of God?' We have to turn away from loving anything more than we love God. That way, we can develop a heart of compassion, a heart that does not harbor any grudge against an offender, and a heart that yearns to be forgiven by God for personal sins.

The prodigal son in our parable study was an idolizer of wealth in that distant country until the severe famine stopped him in his tracks! The Holy Spirit's arrest of his heart when he was down and out was his saving grace. He 'came to his senses' by the grace of God, reversing his beeline trip straight to hell. Indeed, the call to put God first can be daunting if your heart is set on the world. We must agree with the scripture verse from James 1:2 that says 'Consider it pure joy, my brothers and sisters, when you face trials of many kinds because you know that the testing of your faith produces perseverance. Let perseverance finish its work so that you may be mature and complete, not lacking anything.' When we lack nothing, we enter Heaven with many crowns but if our hearts are set on the world, we cannot be forgivers and we will be thrown to our tormentors. 'Forgive as God forgave you' will not come so easy to a person who regards himself as upright. He believes that Heaven is a given. Yet, the number one secret is that Heaven is reserved for those who do not harbor an unforgiving heart. In other words, and in simple terms, if we do not forgive, we cannot go to Heaven. Bible says that we have 'sinned and fall short of the glory of God,' – Romans 3:23, but having been forgiven, we become justified. Heaven is ours, as if our sin never occurred. If we belong to Him through faith in Christ, God does not condemn us for our past sins. Remember again, scripture tells us that our forgiveness from God is conditional upon our forgiving others, 'But if you do not forgive others their sins, your Father will not forgive your sins.' – Matthew 6:15 If we are not forgiving, then we cannot come to God and ask for His forgiveness.

Unforgiven sin therefore surely excludes one from going to Heaven, and not forgiving our offenders mean we have not been forgiven of our own sins. Think about that. It is vital that we develop a profound relationship with Jesus as an important step towards making it to Heaven. This is our Christian mandate as we apply the forgiveness transaction. Since remission of sins go hand in hand with accepting Christ, let us do well to check our status always. Remember also that forgiveness is an act of faith, and refusal to do so is an act of rebellion – against God. We do not even have to wait for the requisite apology. Just as the father in our parable story forgave long before he met his prodigal son, so we also ought to forgive in our hearts and stand ready to enfold. A confession or an apology may make the work easier and if God thinks we need that in order to forgive, He will provide that. Regardless, forgiveness is a God-given phenomenon that must be practiced over and over again in order to secure our reservation to Heaven.

PART B
IN PURSUIT
OF FORGIVENESS

Sometimes we facetiously say in our prayers, 'Oh God forgive me' with obviously no real contrition to God. We say it hurriedly and routinely as part of our ritualistic prayers. If we stopped to consider the power of the words we murmur to God, we would know that He listens keenly, searching our hearts for tiny slivers of brokenness, and when He finds it, He enfolds us into His loving arms. Pursuing divine forgiveness should never be considered a favorite pastime if it has no substance to it. Nor should we see human forgiveness as an attribute of weakness as some may think. As a matter of fact, seeking forgiveness is the most courageous, fulfilling and noble thing to do. Forgiveness from God is an essential facet of our lives that must be taken very seriously. It is beneficial to the soul as we will discover. 2Chronicles 7:14 says 'If my people, who are called by my name, will humble themselves and pray and seek my face and turn from their wicked ways, then I will hear from Heaven and I will forgive their sin and will heal their land.' This verse sums up all we want to study under this new topic – In Pursuit of Forgiveness. We want to learn why we must vigorously pursue forgiveness. God said, if His people, of whom we are part, will humble themselves and pray and seek His face and then turn from our iniquities, then will He forgive us and heal us and restore us. Do come on this journey with me as we critically look at how God grants His forgiveness, how we can pursue it as hard as possible and how we can ensure that we are a forgiven people. Once we are forgiven, we are well on our way to becoming forgiving people.

What does it mean to be in pursuit of forgiveness? Scripture says 'For all have sinned and fall short of the glory of God,' – Romans 3:23 and the verse 25 says 'God presented Christ as a sacrifice of atonement, through the shedding of His blood – to be received by faith.' My interest here is the ending portion of the verse 25, 'to be received by faith.' We need forgiveness from our sins which God has presented ahead of time by the shedding of Christ's blood. To be received by faith is the part we play. We pursue with determination the forgiveness that God already put in place through Christ. It is available, but we have to take it through faith. God offers it, and we take it. Remember the forgiveness transaction we studied from our last section. If we do not take what is on offer, we have not received it. And what are the repercussions? In Ephesians 4:32, the Bible states that 'Be kind and compassionate to one another, forgiving each other, just as Christ God forgave you.' Matthew 6:15, states 'For if you do not forgive others their sins, your Father will not forgive your sins.' Notice the cycle? We ought to forgive, but we ought to seek God's forgiveness for our own forgiveness to be effective. Pursuing or seeking God's forgiveness then, is very important and is an act of humble surrender. It is very essential that we find it in ourselves when we are guilty of any sin, to seek forgiveness quickly so that the favor of God will always be upon us. It is also a factor of trust to seek forgiveness from God as well as from others. This is what forgiveness inquires of us anytime it approaches. That we trust God utterly in our brokenness and that we yearn to be forgiven, so we ask the Holy Spirit to show us how to receive our forgiveness, and not the other way around. Customarily, we tend to show God how He must forgive us, but this should never be the case. We must come to Him broken over our very sins, surrendering them all to Him and then receive His forgiveness by faith. We cannot direct the course of sins against us, but we can benefit vastly from its forgiveness. Once we are forgiven, we are emboldened to do likewise. We can choose to be a victim twice when we are sinned against. Once, for the pain and hurt of the sin itself and twice when we cannot forgive. It is urgent that we learn how to put the burden down and walk away by confronting our own sins and getting them pardoned. It is essential to surrender everything, so that we can release all bitterness and resentment and get our peace. The Prodigal son in our parable is a perfect example of what it takes to seek and receive God's forgiveness. Heartened by this ability, we can then do our forgiveness acts which strengthens us and pleases God.

CHAPTER FIVE
PERFECT SUBMISSION

I. A Contrite Heart
'Perfect submission all is at rest, I in my Savior, am happy and blest, watching and waiting, looking above, filled with his goodness, lost in his love.' -Fanny Crosby9

The hymn writer was on to something when she composed the above song. 'All is at rest,' the hymn says, our guilt and remorse are eliminated when we learn to submit perfectly to God's will. Then we feel happy and blessed as we wait for God to do exploits in our lives. We do not have to worry about our sins again because we are filled with His goodness and His love. What a beautiful portrayal of God's love for mankind. However, God's providence and our passions always run in opposite directions hence our sorrow and pain. Yet when we submit our all to God and foster a heart of contrition, His goodness flows to us and our forgiveness is granted quickly. The prodigal son in our Luke 15 story surely did some deep soul searching. He must have asked himself how he could have been so foolish. How could he have so ruined his life out of pride and ignorance? He considered the wastefulness, the horrid lusts and the resultant misery he was feeling. '...but no one gave him anything' Luke:15:16b of our passage says. How times had changed, he thought. Now he was resorting to begging for a detestable meal of pig pods but even that was denied him. Certainly, he was reaching a point of insanity, and suicide looked pretty good.

While in deep introspection, God laid on his heart a scripture from Nehemiah 9. This lost son remembered the prayer of the Levites, how they cried out to God in a loud voice for the pardon of the sins of Israel and His mercy. With their sins ever before them, they thanked and exalted God and acknowledged the favors He kept bestowing on Israel. The verses 19 and 20 of Nehemiah 9 particularly shook him, 'Because of Your great compassion, You did not abandon them in the wilderness……. You did not withhold manna from their mouths, and You gave them water for their thirst.' Really? Real food instead of food meant for pigs? Would God restore me? As these thoughts raced through his mind, boom! Epiphany! Holy Spirit to the rescue! He 'came to his senses' and so begun his soliloquy; 'how many of my father's hired servants have food to spare and here I am starving to death!' – Luke 15:17 He marveled at the thought since it had not occurred to him before. As understanding dawned, God revealed Himself to him even more. The boy remembered Psalm 86:5-6 'You, Lord are forgiving and good, abounding in love to all who call to You. Hear my prayer, Lord; listen to my cry for mercy.' With tears streaming down his face, contrition washed over our young antagonist like nothing he had ever experienced before. The more the tears poured from his eyes, the greater the pull from God was upon him. Isaiah 55:6 came into his mind to 'Seek the Lord, while He may be found; call on Him while He is near.' Now sorrow and brokenness gripped the prodigal son. He felt the call of God upon him. He knew that if forgiven, he would never venture away from this mighty God. He decided to submit his all to God. He deeply regretted the actions he had taken and wanted forgiveness quickly. He pondered over words of a version of the song 'perfect submission, all is at rest' and he felt a soothing sense of relief and freedom as he looked towards the Heavens.

Friend, a contrite heart is an important condition needed for our overall Christian growth. In contrition, we are crushed because of our sense of guilt over our sins. We recognize that we have committed spiritual crimes against God's laws. When our lives are lived in contrition, God notices and takes particular care of us. Contrition, when defined is the sorrowful regret over sins. It is that pronounced feeling of remorse. In contrition, there are no excuses, no complaints and we never try to defend the reasons behind our sin. Contrition is that intense expression of grief, when we realize that our sins are only against God, at which time we feel intense shame and regret. With all these thoughts flowing into his heart, the prodigal son felt the goodness of the Lord wash over him as he submitted his all to God. This indicates to us that contrition is very critical in the forgiveness process and is motivated by faith and love for God. The son had recognized God's call to seek forgiveness from Him. He had 'come to himself' by the grace of God, and through prayer and reflection he was ready to seek forgiveness. Do we feel that way about our sins, friend? Do we approach God with true brokenness over our sins so He can perform His utmost for us? Every one of us is flawed, bound to sin and in need of forgiveness. Are we ready to submit perfectly and promptly to God? Without contrition, we cannot begin to accept the forgiveness that God has already provided for us. A contrite soul comes about only through faith in God. Psalm 51:16-17 say 'For you will not delight in sacrifice, or I would give it; you will not be pleased with a burnt offering. The sacrifices of God are a broken spirit; a broken and contrite heart, O God, you will not despise.' Contrition and a broken heart help us to completely eschew the sins in our hearts. Without true sorrow of our sin even sacrifices or burnt offerings will not avail forgiveness as the verse above suggests. This shows how heartbroken we must feel about our sins when at the doorstep of God's forgiveness. This is what the prodigal son was feeling. He dared not blame his father nor his older brother. He could not blame the party goers who had helped him spend all his wealth. He knew that this was his and only his act of sin and he was ready to submit his all to God.

God does not despise those who demonstrate contrition because He prompts it in us. He is quick to forgive all who find contrition and express humility and sorrow for a sin.
In Isaiah 43:25, scripture says 'I, and even I, am He who blots out your transgressions, for My own sake and remembers your sins no more.' God is generous and full of grace and mercy. He is ever willing to wipe away all our sins and grant us forgiveness. He is tolerant of us and He seeks us out and causes us to feel contrition so that we can approach Him and receive our forgiveness. As we keep confessing our sins, God forgives us, and this allows us also to forgive our offenders. We suffer great loss when we refuse to forgive because we may feel justified in our resentment and bitterness. Being justified in our resentment is the fastest way to be thrown out to our tormentors. What benefit then is there in that? We cast the blame and criticism on the offender and blind ourselves to the reality of our own faults. This hardens our hearts towards God and makes it impossible to feel contrition for our own sins. To harbor bitterness therefore is unadulterated pride and arrogance and Christ cannot dwell in a heart that feels this way. Let us learn to submit totally to Jesus in all our endeavors. Our burdens will be lightened significantly.

II. Reflecting on our sins
'I will set out and go back to my father and say to him: Father, I have sinned against Heaven and against you. I am no longer worthy to be called your son; make me like one of your hired servants.' - Luke 15:18-19

The main essence of contrition is to reflect on our sins and actions so we can properly submit them all to God. True contrition allows us to see sin as God sees it. God cannot be in the presence of sin. His holiness and sovereignty make it impossible for Him to dwell amid sin. Sin is the antithesis of His very nature. Psalm 5:4 says 'You are not a God who takes pleasure in wickedness; no evil dwells in You.' Holiness is high on the list of God's attributes which makes it impossible for Him to be intimate with sin. God is morally perfect and free from blemish of any kind. When we begin to see sin as the opposite of who God is and what He stands for, contrition over our sins begins to make sense. When Jesus on the Mount of Olives, asked God to spare Him by taking the cup away in Luke 22:42, God had to turn His back on His only begotten son because the load of sin could not be in His presence. His reason for hating sin so much is because it separates us from Him! Imagine that. Such is the depth of His love. As we reflect on our sins, we too realize that it completely separates us from our loving Father. Sin also causes us to be enslaved to the world and to the evil one. Sin will bar us from Heaven and God cannot bear that. God wants us to think about the consequences of our sins as we live our lives. He allows us to reflect over our trespasses so that it dawns on us that 'to be a friend of the world is to show hatred toward God.' – James 4:4 Pondering over the severity of our sins also allow us to place the blame squarely on ourselves. When we see the situation for what it is, we are able to give it all to God in repentance. Forgiveness from God is full and sweet when we have wholly repented.

Taking a look at the prodigal son in the parable of the lost son, his decision in verse 18 of Luke 15, gives us an idea of how we must act when we are overcome by our sins. After God allowed him to 'come to his senses' and sit up, he reflected over all he had done and submitted the sins to God. He must have told God that he was genuinely sorry for how he had acted. Every detail of his life on the run was on his mind. He thought of how he had squandered his wealth in wild living and he felt broken. He thought of his poor father and imagined him up on the roof-top weak and bereft. The prodigal son's heart was broken all over again. Such deep reflection over his wicked ways caused him to weep all over again and he made a firm decision to worship God alone going forward. Friend, what have we learned so far? Are you pained by your sins? Do you even remember your sins? Though some sins are unintentional, others have been pushed far back to the recesses of our hearts and are lodged there. Just as we feel contrition over sins against God, so must we feel remorse over sins against our fellow men, because these are ultimately sins against God. If we have hurt anyone badly, treated them unfairly, pushed them to the brink of frustration, then we owe them repentance and confession. In our moments of reflection, the Holy Spirit will help us recall the sins hidden within us. Psalm 51:3 says 'For I know my transgressions and my sin is always before me. Hide Your face from my sins and blot out all my iniquity.' David had learned about his need for forgiveness very quickly after his transgression. Psalm 51:9 also says 'Then I acknowledged my sin to You and did not cover up my iniquity.' In Psalm 32:5 David said '"I will confess my transgressions to the Lord." And You forgave the guilt of my sin.' As quickly as we 'come to our senses', so we ought to put all ego aside and cry out to God in genuine repentance. The significance is not so much the gravity of our sin, but what we are willing to do about them. For if we refuse to be forgiven for our own sins, we grieve the Spirit of God. Let us allow the

Holy Spirit to fill our hearts as we reflect on our sins and become contrite over them. Let us seek out our victims, just as we seek God out to repent. We should repent and seek their forgiveness, just as we do with God. Then we can pursue God's forgiveness with all our might. Do not let sin get in the way of a beautiful relationship with God and our fellow men because there are no benefits in sin. God knows that we cannot become holy all by ourselves, because sin is always 'crouching at our doors to which we must rule over.' – Genesis 4:7b, but He promises to help us in our struggle against sin, 'keep us firm to the end, so that you will be blameless.' – 1Corinthians 1:8 Let us do all we can then to live a forgiven life so that we will be in God's presence forevermore.

III. Facing your sin
'If we claim to be without sin, we deceive ourselves and the truth is not in us.' -1John 1:8

Our young antagonist the prodigal son, sat in the pig-pen, lonely and desperate and took a good look at sins he committed against God and felt disdain for each of them. He recollected the arrogance with which he addressed his family, and the pride that had overtaken him completely. He thought about all the horrible deeds he had committed with his fake friends in the distant country and he understood that he had allowed himself to die. A spiritual death, with no feeling to trespasses, no relationship with Christ, cut off from family and friends and certainly destitute. He grieved in his heart for each of these sins, not just because he was contrite, but because he knew that God was also grieving in His heart over every single sin as well. God's heart was deeply troubled to the point of regret over our sinful nature and wasted years – Genesis 6:6. For that matter, it is important that we make the decision to face our sins squarely and repent of them so God can forgive us. Sin may look attractive and enticing when Christ is not in the picture. The devil might convince us that our behavior may not even be sin. But the Bible says in 1John 1:9-10 'If we confess our sins, He is faithful and just and will forgive us our and purify us from all unrighteousness. If we claim we have not sinned, we make Him out to be a liar and His word is not in us.' We should never allow the evil one to diminish the seriousness of our sin in any way. For our God is not a liar – Numbers 23:19. We need His Word in us so we can live holy and acceptable lives. Forgiveness is too much of a valuable gift to be taken for granted. It demands so much from us, yet when received or extended, it is the most beautiful phenomenon. This is revealed in our story when the prodigal son trembled at the sins he had committed. He hardly knew how to take them to the Lord in prayer, but the Holy Spirit quickened his faith and, in his contrition and desire to make amends, he prayed this confession prayer thus to God, 'I have sinned against You and only You, and I am truly saddened by my sins, forgive me Heavenly Father, and take away my burdens.' We must never play down our sins or hide them or wish them away. We must face each of these sins head-on, viewing them as they are, as ugly as they may appear and talk boldly to them. We must hate the very idea that we sinned against God in the manner we did. This is the initial step of seeking forgiveness from God, for when we do not, we just deceive ourselves and forgiveness will not be our portion.

The other reason why we have to look at our sins critically and understand the nature and magnitude of them is so that we can vow never to go in that direction again. Upon reflection, the prodigal son could not believe all that he had done. Where did the audacity to be so rude come from? Why did he squander away his life the way he did? As he examined and marked off each sin, he cried out unto the Lord to take each and every one of them away forever. Likewise, when we sin, we lose our perception of forgiveness and our sense of peace with God. So, as we pray and confess our sins, by the enablement of the Holy Spirit, we are rekindled into awareness of the work of the cross and God uses that to revive us and assure us of our salvation. Friend, let us continue to pray daily for forgiveness of sin. We must do so with the confidence that comes from the knowledge that we are in a covenant relationship with God. He will forgive us always on the basis of the work of Jesus on the cross.

IV. Emptiness of Self
'Do your best to present yourself to God as one approved, a worker who does not need to be ashamed, and who correctly handles the word of truth.' - 2Timothy 2:15

The processes of contrition, reflection and prayer allow us to empty self entirely of sins and receive God's forgiveness. The burden of sin is rolled away at the feet of His forgiveness. As forgiveness looks on with joy, ready to embrace, the Heavenly host begin celebrations. What an awesome time it is when we receive this humbling gift from God. He stood ready all along and finally here we are, truly forgiven. We have 'come to our senses' by the grace of God and by faith we recognized our sin for what it was, blaming no one and accepting all our faults. We were burdened by our sins and contrition set in. Our deep sorrow sent us to our knees in desperation. All we could see was the precious blood of Jesus, the agony He endured as He shouted 'it is finished' on the cross. We prayed out loud, worshipping God almighty and confessing our sins, all jumbled together. God always knows what to do with our genuine prayers. He in His sovereignty, is able to distinguish them all, placing each where they belong. He is also wondrously able to separate the load of sin from us, His beloved. Then as we sense the assurance of His forgiveness, we feel empty, broken, alive and excited, and it dawns on us that God has really taken our burden of sin and rolled it all away. Now we can fill our emptiness with the fruit of the Spirit 'love, joy, peace, forbearance, kindness, goodness, faithfulness, gentleness and self-control.' – Galatians 5:22 When we go to our victims in repentance, it must never be a half-hearted effort; we sincerely confess and repent to them and know that God through them will forgive us.

Friend, can you imagine the journey back home for the prodigal son? His feeble gait back home was not all due to hunger. He felt light and empty mainly because the burden of sin had been rolled away forever. He was a forgiven soul and he could not wait to get back home with his new lease on life. He planned on telling the servants about the love of God and the need to forgive and be forgiven. He also planned on a special union with his older brother, when he would seek his forgiveness as well. It is about time we took that bold step of faith and sought our forgiveness from God and also from man. Being forgiven by God brings all kinds of possibilities. Not only are we emptied of all our sins, but now we can also forgive our offenders and be assured of our place in the Kingdom of God.

CHAPTER SIX
AN ACT OF
SURRENDER

I. Surrender defined
'For to me to live is Christ and to die is gain.'
-Philippians 1:21

The word 'Surrender' is a military term which means to 'give oneself up', to 'cease resisting to an adversary' and submit to their authority. There are many times we shun God's capture because we do not want to surrender our all to Him. Yet, we are duty bound as Christian soldiers, having been purchased by the blood of Jesus and redeemed from sin to be disciplined by grace and to make God a priority. The battle between our will and the will of God must end in us waving the flag of surrender each time, but due to our sinful and selfish nature, this battle is never ending. Right off the bat, I must state that our motive for surrender should not be for personal gain. Usually when we need something, we surrender to God, but once received, we fall off track. Authentic surrender is that which is for Christ and His sovereignty only.

In the Greek language, to surrender is 'paradidomi' 10 which means 'to yield up' or 'entrust'. This suggests a total giving up of ourselves and a deep cleaving to God. Biblical surrender means we no longer transmit our will or our worries and desires to another person but instead, we look upward to God and humbly tell Him to take over our lives completely. We surrender by entrusting all that belongs to us to God. We know that He has our best interests at heart so we leave all our cares with Him. Surrender will be tough when attempted with our own strength. The thought of giving up our own will and deeds to the will of God does not come easy. Often times we say to the Lord 'Let Your will be done' but what we really mean is 'Lord let Your will become what I will.' Matthew 16:24-25, shows us our instruction list of how to surrender to the authority of God. 'Then Jesus told His disciples, 'If anyone would come after Me, let him deny himself and take up his cross and follow Me. For whoever would save his life will lose it, but whoever loses his life for My sake will find it.' This passage identifies several steps that leads us to a surrendered life. 'If anyone would come after me' is the initial invitation of surrender. The prodigal son received this invitation when he was sent out to the fields by a citizen of the distant country to feed pigs. Luke 15:15. He needed that isolation, the quietness that stilled the clanging noise of his selfish pride. He was desolate and miserable and the sharp contrast was just what he needed to turn his life around. As he walked the fields, and fed the pigs, the contrast of his life at home and life now hit him hard. This was the invitation to go back to God. God had invited him to leave that which was foreign to his mentality and accept that which would make him whole again. This initial step of surrender is not easy. Though the son was traumatized by his very existence, his stubborn heart and pride made it difficult for him to surrender immediately. Next, in the instruction verses above, Jesus calls for self-denial. 'Let him deny himself,' Jesus says, and if we would do this with everything we have in our quest to surrender, God's wonderful plan for our lives would unfold joyfully. Needless to say, our young antagonist also fought this tooth and nail. When the severe famine broke out in the distant country, Luke 15:14, he did not immediately consider going back to his loving family. He was not ready to submit his will and embrace God. Perhaps he thought, 'this famine will end soon and I can go back to my ways'. He was still living his life on his own terms, disastrous as that was. He could not immediately deny himself. In the next step of these instruction verses, Matthew 16:24:25, Jesus mentions taking up ones' cross. Taking up our cross would mean swallowing our pride and admitting that we are wrong and commit to a humble and changed life, living as Christ did. The prodigal son was not ready to surrender to the perfect model of Christ just yet. His self-will had a tight grip over him, and he was evading God's capture with all he had, forgetting that all earthly things eventually fade away at the expense of forfeiting that which God had for him. Finally, in this Matthew 16 instruction scripture, Christ asks us to follow Him. Eventually, this son gave up control when he came to his senses by the grace of God. He left the uncertainty of his miserable life and took a bold step towards security and love. To be dedicated followers of Christ takes all our strength and wisdom, but more significantly, it requires us to surrender control of our very lives.

Friend, we must surrender our will to God because He has created each of us for a specific purpose and the further we stray from Him, the closer we get to being thrown to our tormentors. The rest of the verse 25 of Matthew 16 says 'For whoever would save his life will lose it, but whoever loses his life for My sake will find it.' It sure was with great joy that the prodigal son set off back to his father. He had surrendered his life to God, had been forgiven and was prepared to let God lead him going forward. God is trustworthy and loving and He knows the end from the beginning and has a plan to prosper us and not to harm us. Jesus set the example by surrendering to God in prayer. In the garden of Gethsemane, Jesus prayed 'not my will but Yours be done.' – Luke 22:42 Once we decide to surrender our will to Christ, faith becomes our proclivity. We remember the work of the cross every day, and God loves and honors a life that is surrendered to Him. He rewards that life with the greatest fulfillment imaginable. In our pursuit of forgiveness, we must be ready to surrender everything we are unto the Lord. This is succinctly portrayed in Judson Van DeVenter's11 hymn, 'All to Jesus I surrender, all to Him I freely give. I will always love and trust Him in His hands securely live. I surrender all, all to Him my blessed savior I surrender all.' Let us then approach God in perfect surrender as we yearn for forgiveness of our sins. When our hearts are malleable and surrendered, we are better inclined to repent of our sins and receive the forgiveness that God has put on the table.

II. The work of Humility
'Humble yourselves, therefore, under the mighty hand of God, that He may lift you up in due time.' - 1Peter 5:6

Humility is a beautiful word in the Christian realm because it is the nature of God. It is not merely an outward disposition but the very attitude of ones' heart. Humility simply means we recognize and submit to God's will in all our endeavors. By humility, we acknowledge that God did not create us so we can glorify self, but for His own glorification. Humility is able to transform hearts, while reminding us to recognize God as the source and giver of everything we have. Humility and forgiveness are vigorously portrayed in the life of Jesus, and are essential characteristics in the Heavenly realm because both show the need for subordination to God. Humility therefore always gives the credit to God. 1Corinthians 1:31 says 'Let the one who boasts, boast in the Lord.' God delivers people who humble themselves before Him and that is the reason we want to learn about humility. In humility, we acknowledge our lack of merit and our inability to save ourselves. In humility we live our lives with the work of the cross ever before us, never forgetting that Christ exchanged our sins for His righteousness and our insignificance for His infinite worth. Humility thus always calls for obedience.

As we pursue forgiveness, it is as though we are pursuing humility and obedience. It necessitates us obediently approaching God in humble contrition, brokenness and surrender. Then we tell God that He is bigger than our problems and that He can solve them better than we ever can, and we also acknowledge His might and His power in humility. In Proverbs 3:34 and James 4:6, the Bible says 'God gives grace to the humble but resists the proud.' Further, if we want God's grace, we have to be humble. The prodigal son in our parable had to learn this lesson quickly. He endured hardship for a while, but after confessing all his sins to the Lord, God's grace came upon him. Again, we learn from Luke 14:11 that 'if we exalt ourselves, we are in opposition to God, who will humble us. But if we humble ourselves, He gives us more grace and exalts us.' If we are proud, God will have to humble us, and it will not be a good thing, but if we have a humble stance, God will exalt us. 1Peter 5:6 says 'Humble yourselves therefore, under God's mighty hand, that He may lift you up in due time.' Apostle Paul is a good example of humility that is graced with godly exaltation. Paul exclaims in 1Timothy 1:15 that Jesus Christ came into the world to save sinners of whom he Paul is the worst. By humbling himself and elevating Christ's worth in his endeavors, Paul experienced the lifting up of God, not for himself, but to stage God's glory. He maintained an attitude of deference towards God and others and in humility always put Christ and others ahead of his own interests. It is important that we also measure everything in terms of God's will, so He exalts us. Based on all the descriptions above, we realize that if humility is not in the mix, we cannot even begin to seek forgiveness from God nor from others. Since it is His will that we seek His forgiveness and extend it to others, we must humbly and genuinely obey.

The father in our parable from Luke 15 portrayed humility amazingly. As devastating as the news from his younger son was, he did not throw a temper tantrum when he heard it, nor did he react negatively to the insolence of his son. Instead, he recalled all the scripture verses that he knew on obedience, forgiveness and humility. Philippians 2:5-8 particularly stuck out, as he envisaged the humble mindset of Jesus even unto death for mankind. This father was also determined that the work of the cross would not be in vain. With the backing of the Holy Spirit, and a humble attitude, father succeeded in separating the sin from his son, and instant forgiveness ensued in his heart. This demonstrates to us how our posture must always exhibit humility as we model our savior Jesus. We are admonished to have Christ's mindset, who did not consider equality with God as something to be used to his own advantage, but made himself nothing, and took on the nature of a servant. Now why all this? If we want to live a blessed and fruitful life, we need to be humble and likewise we ought to have a humble spirit if we want God's forgiveness. It is imperative that we swallow our pride and see God as King of kings. This is the key to our pursuit of forgiveness. Putting the will of God ahead of ours, always. It does take great inner strength and obedience to be humble, and that is how we validate our focus on God. We need humility in order to always recognize our need for God's forgiveness, so let us surrender ourselves to the work of humility and obedience. Humble people recognize that they are servants to everyone. Having a humble spirit is not easy because our sinful nature is always trying to express itself and get in the way of our quest to seek God genuinely. 'For the flesh desires what is contrary to the spirit, and the spirit what is contrary to the flesh.' – Galatians 5:17 As such it takes a steadfast heart to remain humble, and it is achievable. In 1Corinthians 9:27, we are admonished to beat the body into submission so we are not disqualified from the race. Another reason for humility is that it is the antithesis of the evil one. Satan's best characteristic is pride, for which he was expelled from his Heavenly position. He does not submit to God and all he does is try to steal, kill and destroy. We must do all we can never to acquiesce to pride because it is of the devil. Let us stand out and exercise true humility which is rooted in the life of Christ. Jesus Christ underwent persecution, but endured it with the knowledge that God would exalt Him. Friend, stay on course in your quest to be humble. It takes courage and constant awareness and work, yet it circumvents pride if we do not give up. It is the only way we can remain forgiven and be forgivers. Colossians 3:12 says 'Therefore as God's chosen people, holy and dearly loved, clothe yourselves with compassion, kindness, humility, gentleness and patience.'

III. The Prayer Quotient
'And you will seek me and find me, when you search for me with all your heart' - Jeremiah 29:13

Matthew 7:7 says 'Ask and it shall be given, seek and you will find, open and it will be opened to you.' In James 4:2, Bible says 'You do not have because you do not ask.' Prayer is simply communicating with God. It is also an acknowledgement to God of our helpless state, and a reaching out to Him to send us our needed help. The above Bible verses tell us that God is personal and He cares for us. He yearns to hear from us in prayer. Search for Me, seek for Me and ask Me, He always says. He is keen to have a communication relationship with His children. However, He does not enforce submission in prayer but gives us the free will to choose to call upon Him anytime. In prayer, we are able to tell God that we love Him and want to be in His presence always. Prayer allows us to be obedient and humble. When we pray a heartfelt prayer to God, He lovingly shows us our shortcomings and helps us to overcome them. Connecting directly with God is something we cannot do without. 'Submit yourselves then to God, Resist the devil and he will flee.' – James 4:7

As we submit to God in prayer, it is important to note the difference between requests and demands. The prodigal son in our parable was good at demanding everything before he had an encounter with God. He demanded his share of the inheritance. He would pompously dictate his needs to family and friends without a care, so it came as a shock to him when he became destitute. When he 'came to his senses' and learned to surrender to God, his prayer mode took on a different note. God graciously allowed the boy to meditate on this verse in Philippians 4:6 'Do not be anxious about anything but in prayer and supplication, with thanksgiving, present your requests to God.' This son was now able to quietly communicate his predicament, requesting forgiveness from God in a humble manner and leaving God to deal with the situation with His own superior wisdom. The boy's tone was no longer brash and demanding. He prayed 'Not my will dear Lord, but Your will be done.' Even he the prodigal, marveled at how far grace had brought him. He wanted to shout to the whole world that we serve a living and loving God who forgives our sins when we seek Him humbly and diligently.

Submitting to God in prayer as we seek forgiveness is therefore very crucial. God commands that we pray. Bible says to 'devote ourselves to prayer, being watchful and thankful,' – Colossians 4:2, and 1Thessalonians 5:7 adds 'pray continually.' Prayer is an act of obedience – and when God commands, we must respond promptly. We get our cue from Jesus who prayed regularly. His prayer life was an example to us so we could learn to do same. Prayer is also the means by which we make confession of all sins, and it truly is the only way we can pursue God's forgiveness. Such a time helps us to repent genuinely and flee from a life of sin, and God grants us power over evil when we call upon Him in prayer. Imagine what the father in our story could have done when he saw such disrespect in his younger prodigal son. Yet his silent prayer to God helped him overcome all the ill-feelings he could have harbored in his heart towards his son.

Friend, nothing can keep us from approaching God in prayer except our own choices. Let us choose to pray about everything, whatever we do, whatever situation we find ourselves in, let us just submit to God in prayer for, if we do not submit in prayer, we are lost. We need to experience God on a personal level, and submitting to Him in prayer will help us achieve that. Prayer will also strengthen our relationship with others and help us receive forgiveness and grant same to our offenders more easily. Prayer will always succeed when all other means fail. Do submit then to God in prayer, and your burdens will surely roll away.

IV. The Role of Fasting
'So we fasted and petitioned our God about this, and He answered our prayer.' - Ezra 8:23

To 'fast' is derived from a word that means 'to cover the mouth', telling us not to nourish the body through our mouths. Fasting is a physical endeavor with deep spiritual connotations that allow us to draw close to God, to understand His purpose for us, to change our nature and to keep us humble. Fasting makes us aware of our sins and helps us cultivate a hunger for God's Word, His righteousness and will. Fasting is a time when we turn off our physical appetites and abide in the bosom of the spirit of God. During this time, secret sins are brought to light and we have a natural inclination to seek God's forgiveness. We instinctively become more sensitive to His conviction and more aware of areas of disobedience in our lives. In Isaiah 58, we learn how seriously God takes our fasting. If we fast in a lackadaisical manner, God is not pleased. When we fast and we feed on the Word and submit totally to God, reflecting on His purpose and will for us, He lifts all our burdens and helps us to walk a righteous walk.

So how does fasting help us in our pursuit of forgiveness? The connection between fasting and forgiveness is that, as we draw closer to God in fasting and prayer:
We are naturally more likely to seek forgiveness.
Contrition and repentance come more easily when we lay down our stomachs, because the Holy Spirit joins with us in our lightened state to express our thoughts to God.
If we find it difficult to shake our guilt to seek God's forgiveness, a fast will rescue us from this predicament.

We ask Him to show us our hearts, to shine His Spirit on to us and reveal that which is hidden so that we can ask Him to forgive us.

Fasting brings us discernment since God sees the humility in the fast and then proceeds to speak to our hearts.

Fasting helps us to understand certain problems better, in order to solve them.

In the case of Daniel in Daniel 9:3, Bible says 'I set my face towards the Lord God to make a request by prayer and supplications, with fasting, sackcloth and ashes, and I prayed to the Lord my God, and made confession.' Daniel knew that a sincere fast would produce quick results and answers from God. The same is seen with Queen Esther in the Bible book of Esther 4:16.

In our pursuit of forgiveness, there is no time to waste. Fasting will allow us to humbly confess all our sins so that our forgiveness will be quick. Fasting will teach us how to petition God in the right manner, because obedience and humility will always present themselves with fasting. It is a good thing to get into fasting mode when we seek forgiveness, because the fear associated with confessing our enormous sins are cut out when we fast. God sends His special angels to assist our every need when He sees our dedicated fast. As such when we fast, we tell God that we yearn to worship Him more, we want to live clean obedient lives and we want to abide under His will at all times. Our parable of the Lost Son has a rich reservoir of reasons why fasting during hardship is important. The father in our story probably spent countless hours up on his roof-top fasting and praying. He must have called unto God to forgive him for his sins, the sins of his two sons and his household amidst fasting. He undoubtedly humbled himself in obedience and swore to God that he would enfold his younger son in his arms and celebrate him when God granted him forgiveness. As we know from the story, his desires were met because of his humble, gentle and obedient spirit. The younger son must have been undertaking his own fasting period too. After his catastrophic experience in a distant country, we see him being drawn to this verse in scripture, 'Even now,' declares the Lord, 'return to me with all your heart, with fasting and weeping and mourning.' – Joel 2:12 It surely cut him to the core and he humbly cried out to the Lord in a fast as he sought forgiveness. God was pleased and pardoned him. His fasting had locked down his contrition and he did not despair nor did he have second thoughts about ever going back to his old ways. Fasting will always lock in our prayers, and the forgiveness that we seek. Let us yearn to surrender to God in fasting. He will quickly hear us and help us.

CHAPTER SEVEN
REPENTANCE MODE

I. What is Repentance?
'Repent, then and turn to God, so that your sins may be wiped out, that times of refreshing may come from the Lord.'
- Acts 3:19

A simple definition for repentance is to turn from sin. It is when we change our minds entirely about the sin that has so consumed us. Not only are our minds changed, but the actions following will prove that we no longer want to associate with the sin. It is a complete turn from evil to good and it comes with demonstration of a new attitude. Luke 3:8 says 'you produce fruit in keeping with repentance.' As such, when we make the conscious decision based on sorrow and regret for our sins, our actions must prove so. The Greek word for repentance is 'metanoia' 12, which means to change or shift perspective. Repentance means not only are we saying we are sorry because we recognize that our previous actions were wrong and violated God's holiness but we also say that we desire to make them right going forward. Furthermore, repentance brings about a change in our outlook and how we think about God. His sovereignty takes on new meaning for a repented soul. We want to be holy and we want to do God's will. It is almost as if we want to make up for lost time because the godly sorrow has overwhelmed us.

We cannot look at repentance without looking at faith, because we cannot place faith in Jesus without changing our minds about our prior sins. Biblical repentance always brings salvation because we now embrace Christ rather than reject Him. Yet we must realize that we do not repent to earn this salvation. It is God who gives us that pull towards Himself. Repentance is God-given, and is by grace alone. John 6:44 says 'No one can come to Me unless the Father who sent Me draws them.' No one can repent by themselves unless God grants them repentance. The prodigal son in our Luke 15 story makes us very aware of the behind the scenes work God does. From the verse 14, when the severe famine hit the distant country, to the time he came to his senses in the pig-pen and repented, we glimpse that it had to have been God working to save him. This boy knew the way home, and could have picked himself up and gone back home at the first signs of the famine. With his nature, he would not have had any problem ransacking his home with arrogance and pride, stepping on everyone to do his bidding again. Yet, for him to receive his repentance, God had him stay! He stayed in the distant country long enough for the severe famine to affect him, he stayed long enough to need a job, he tried to look for a job (surely not a one-day event), he eventually found a job that he hated, he was on the verge of starvation, almost collapsing in his need. All of a sudden, God draws him in. 'And when he came to himself,' the King James Bible puts it aptly. Scripture did not say 'then he came to his senses' or 'soon he came to his senses.' Instead it says 'and when' this suggests pull and tag, a back and forth, a passage of time. This dynamic tells us that there must have been confusion in the prodigal's stubborn heart. With this verse, we believe that the argument was over. He had received what God was granting to His beloved soul. God had used the difficult circumstances to slowly draw him, open his eyes and change his heart. God's longsuffering had led our boy to repentance. 2Peter 3:9 says 'the Lord is not slow in keeping His promise, as some understand slowness. Instead He is patient with you, not wanting anyone to perish, but everyone to come to repentance.' What a mighty God we serve! He summons us to unconditional surrender so we can confess and repent of our sins. He is eager to forgive us so we can also extend forgiveness to others.

Friend, we should not despair when we go through trials of many kinds, consider it pure joy the Bible says, since it makes us persevere, mature and helps us to lack nothing. James 1:2-4. Our young prodigal, thus felt that pull after much desolation and he responded inwardly at first, pleading with God to forgive and deliver him from the burden of sin and fear of judgment. He vowed at that instant to change his heart, his behavior and his purpose. His heart was broken over his sins and as they lay bare before him, they looked repulsive. So it is with true repentance, we earnestly want a turnaround, not just to relieve any pain, but to have a clean heart and right spirit before God. We sincerely ask God to open our eyes to see ourselves as we are and recognize our sinful ways and make a turn around. When that happens, oh what a joy! For the way we view things change. It does not just mean feeling bad over our prior bad behavior, but it becomes more about feeling awe and delight towards God as we glimpse His power and glory. Yet, as repentance works its miracles in our hearts, we have to be careful against attrition.

Attrition is when one's contrition is not real. It is also known as false repentance. In this case, the sorrow one feels for one's sins is based on the fear of punishment or sorrow from getting caught. Judas in Matthew 27:3 did show remorse, but he did not turn from his sin to ask for forgiveness. There was no spiritual turning, because he lacked the faith needed to repent. We need the Holy Spirit to produce real sorrow for sin in our hearts. Psalm 32:2-5, shows us a vivid picture of how repentance draws in God's forgiveness. 'Blessed is the one whose sin the Lord does not count against them and in whose spirit is no deceit. When I kept silent, my bones wasted away through my groaning all day long. For day and night Your hand was heavy on me; my strength was sapped as in the heat of summer. Then I acknowledged my sin to You and did not cover up my iniquity. I said, "I will confess my transgressions to the Lord." And You forgave the guilt of my sin.' God is able to wash away our iniquity when we come to Him in true repentance. Let us keep our eyes on God alone. He will help us in our pursuit of forgiveness.

II. Forgive Thyself
'Cast all your anxieties on Him, because He cares for you.'
-1Peter 5:7
Interestingly, the Bible does not specifically refer to self-forgiveness, yet it is very essential in the repentance process. No matter how much one has been released from sin's bondage and forgiven by God, or how much one has forgiven his or her offender, it is not unusual for some to flounder in unresolved guilt. Sometimes we believe that self-forgiveness is not even a concern because we think we must continuously recall our forgiven sins lest we forget its gravity. By so doing, we separate ourselves from God because that in itself is a sin. It is true that shame and self-contempt may cause us to be unable to forgive ourselves but this does not help us in our Christian living because it is a form of pride. We say to God: Your grace is not powerful enough to wipe clean this sin. We feel we have to do something big to feel or earn His forgiveness. This is a lie from the devil who whispers to us that we are still guilty of our sin and should always feel that way. The accuser of our souls thus always has a field day when our

guilt persists and we are unable to get past our sin to feel forgiven. He stirs up old emotions - making us anxious and desperate. Alas, several of us are unable to 'forgive ourselves' after God's amazing forgiveness has been bestowed upon us. Such people do not move beyond their past because intriguingly, they do not want to let go of their former sins. They may actually get a displaced thrill out of re-living past sins in their minds. Wallowing in past sins, or throwing a pity-party gives them a weird sense of assurance of not being in danger of going to hell. Our Bible reminds us in 2Corinthians 5:17 that 'Therefore if anyone is in Christ, he is a new creation. The old has passed away; behold, the new has come.' When we repented, confessed and were forgiven we immediately became a new creation in Christ Jesus. We need never re-visit our past sinful life anymore. God has forgiven us in advance by the work done on the cross at Calvary. It is important that we do not buy in to the 'I'm not worthy, woe is me' adage, and forgive ourselves so we can be of service to the Kingdom of Heaven. If God has willingly done so much for us, the least we can do is free ourselves and our offenders from our hearts as well.

As mentioned, maintaining in our hearts and minds past sins that have already been forgiven is actually a new sin. It says of us that we really do not trust God, and we have to work out our forgiveness all by ourselves. Proverbs 16:25 says 'there is a way that seems right to a man, but its end is the way of death.' Friend, if you are holding a grudge against your own self, but you have encountered God in repentance before, know that your way is not right. That energy it takes to harbor anger, guilt and resentment of self, robs us of the joy that God would want us to receive in being forgiven. As such, proclaiming a separate set of rules and values for ourselves than that which God sets, shows that we have rejected God's mercy and we are headed towards self-destruction. Forgiving self does not justify the sin we committed, but it shows our humility to God in believing that He alone can wash away our sins. It is courageous to do so and it gives us strength to rise up from becoming a victim. The prodigal son would have been a perfect example of a person who would wallow in his ego. Self-pity, self-importance and certainly inability to forgive himself for anything due to arrogance and pride. Yet, God captured his heart completely because God knew this lad needed deep forgiveness. The prodigal son only recalled his sins in order to get past them once and for all. Self-forgiveness should remind us of the great Savior who forgave us, undeserving though we will always be, and drew us closer in loving obedience to Him.

In our endeavor to maintain a repentant stance, let us forgive ourselves, so God's forgiveness can take full effect in us and our healing can begin. For when we forgive ourselves, it is easier to cultivate a spirit of forgiveness too because we have that sense of joy, peace and freedom that comes from receiving God's forgiveness. Don't believe the devil's lie that you are still guilty so you must act guilty. It is a sin to do that. Let us forsake re-living our sins, because it just makes us sin all over again. We are determined to take it to the Lord in prayer and be forgiven for 'there is therefore now no condemnation for those who are in Christ Jesus.' – Romans 8:1

III. Mercy: An Enigma
'And he passed in front of Moses, proclaiming, The Lord, The Lord, the compassionate and gracious God, slow to anger, abounding in love and faithfulness, maintaining love to thousands, and forgiving wickedness, rebellion and sin. Yet He

does not leave the guilty unpunished; He punishes the children and their children for the sin of the parents to the third and fourth generation. Moses bowed to the ground at once and worshipped.'
-Exodus 34: 6-8

So far, we have looked at repentance mainly from the human point of view; what we have to do, and how we must feel as we pursue God's forgiveness. Let us not get ahead of ourselves in thinking we achieve God's forgiveness by our own efforts. Whatever we accomplish during the repentance process can only transpire when God's mercy comes to the rescue. God's mercy is an enigma; a unique mystery that can emerge at any instance to work mighty wonders. A quick study of Exodus 34:6-8 quoted above points this out perfectly. In this Bible passage, we meet God, willing to renew His covenant relationship with the Israelites even though they had failed Him many times. Moses had come back to meet Him at Mount Sinai on behalf of His people. Our amazing God introduces Himself to Moses and describes who He is. He is Yahweh, meaning 'Whatever I AM, I will be', and just in case the greatness of His Name did not sink in, He spells it out again. He is sovereign and changes not, whatever He is, He always is. Then He tells Moses about His compassion, grace and abounding love, bringing the magnificence of His mercy into full view. Time and again, His beloved people – the Israelites showed disdain towards Him but He held back His wrath because of His grace and mercy. Indeed, we give Him abundant reasons to be angry at all times because of our iniquities, yet He abounds in steadfast love and mercy. This mercy is seen throughout the Bible. Adam and Eve failed Him, His beloved people of Israel failed Him again and again, and we fail Him too, but God is still merciful. This part of scripture solidifies God's faithfulness towards us. After deep rebellion, unbelief, complaints, idolatry, God did not cast out His people. He spelled out that forgiveness is for the repentant soul, but the refusal of forgiveness is for those who are unrepentant. In the verse 7 of the above quotation, He tells us Himself that He forgives iniquity, transgression and sin. All manner of sin will be forgiven if we repent. That is it! Yet He cannot clear the guilty who do not turn and repent! Remember that He is a just God and will right every wrong. He will not ignore the evils that are done. He lifted our sins unto Himself and died on the cross because that is what His forgiveness does. Our sins have been separated from us and removed by His own death on the cross.

To illustrate further, the prodigal son in our parable was guilty of many sins, but once he accepted the promptings from the Holy Spirit to repent, his sins were pardoned quickly and he received his forgiveness. We are in the same predicament friend, rebellious, unbelieving, and idolatrous. When we are unrepentant, God considers it as hatred of Him, so our iniquities will be visited on our descendants. On the other hand, anyone who truly repents and turns from sin is quickly forgiven because of God's mercy through the shed blood of Jesus. In many ways God in His mercy prompts us to repent and be forgiven. We are assured that when we return to God with contrition and a broken heart over our iniquities, He graciously forgives because He is merciful. This is what He always wanted for His people – to be repentant so He can show His mercy. The measure of His love is found on the Calvary cross, when our savior Jesus Christ came to confirm and seal the mercies of God by dying for our sins. He is the lamb of God, the only way to God's forgiveness. Christ is the enigma of God's mercies. Let us listen out for Him, look to that cross and not our conditions as the measure of God's faithfulness towards us and repent. In the verse 8 of Exodus 34, we read that 'And Moses bowed to the ground and worshipped at once!' He was awestruck by the magnificence of God, His compassion, grace, love and above all, the enigma and majesty of His mercy.

In order for us to be merciful to others, we also must bow down as Moses did, in joyful worship of our enigmatic Savior. We must constantly be reflecting on God's abundant mercy, for when we were at our lowest, contemplating pig pods like the prodigal son, He met us and offered us abundant life in Him. He brought Himself low, demonstrating the depth of His steadfast love, faithfulness and mercies by taking on the form of a servant and dying on the cross at Calvary for us. This is the reason we pursue forgiveness, that we can also apply the mercies of Christ in forgiveness to others to the glory of God.

IV. A New Mindset
'Then I acknowledged my sin to You and did not cover up my iniquity. I said, "I will confess my transgressions to the Lord." And You forgave the guilt of my sin.' - Psalm 32:5

The prodigal son had a dilemma. After his near miss attempt at eating pig pods, and him coming to himself, a radical sensation was taking place in his inner soul, and he did not know what to make of it. His eyes had been opened and he was precipitously jarred with the dreadfulness of his wickedness and rebellion that had been in his heart for a long time which he had taken for granted. Now, he felt within him that he hated his old way of thinking and acting. He needed a major mindset change, because his frame of mind was all over the place, and he knew within him that a new outlook was now his portion and things had to change fast. With all that crying, and the deep contrition and brokenness over his offenses, he knew that a new godly stance was nigh. Our counsellor and friend the Holy Spirit was softly and gently encouraging our young antagonist to confess all his sins to God, who had been waiting all along for this time. He was being urged to have the same mindset as Christ and become humble. This would help him, the Holy Spirit continued, to turn himself around in his effort to make changes to his life. Upon receipt, our young prodigal was contrite all over again and with gigantic tears in his eyes, he confessed his sins in profound repentance to God and joy was restored. 'This,' Holy Spirit whispered to him, 'is your key to forgiveness.'

Our pursuit of forgiveness must necessarily bring about a changed mindset. This new mindset allows us to see our own helplessness and the need to leave our lives of sin forever. We need to consult with the Holy Spirit who tenderly helps us through our confession and repentance. King David is a great example of how to rise up from sins and embrace confession and repentance. The Bathsheba story, pronounces his repentance process and it is an inspiration to all Christians, since it beautifully sums up all that we have studied in this chapter so far. Psalm 51 is a psalm of a changed heart. There is sincere confession of all his sins. David pleads with God to have mercy on him according to God's loving kindness. Yet his plea for forgiveness from God was grounded on God's faithfulness and love and not on the merits of David. In the first two verses, David turns to God and pleads with Him, asking God to wash away all his iniquity. In verse 3, David faces the ugliness of his sins, admits that he willfully committed them and is aghast at the extent of these sins. He acknowledges that all sin is actually against God, and for that he shows true remorse. His guilt and plea are very evident and heartfelt in the next two verses where he admits that his sinfulness was from birth. In the sixth verse he passionately pleads for renewal and asks that only God can make him clean again. He then asks God for a new heart in verse 10 and once more begs not to be cast away from God's presence. In the verses that follow, he continues with his plea and asks for a new life – a mindset change and a total turn around.

Friend, this is what we hope for as we pursue God's forgiveness. We must open ourselves to the Holy Spirit's conviction with joy, and purposefully pour out our hearts unto the Lord in deep confession and repentance. As we commit to turning over our wayward lives, God floods our heart with newness, godly sorrow and joy with the help of the Holy Spirit. This is the only way our repentance will take hold. With this changed mind-set, we must not let up. It is important that we appropriate our forgiven state every single day, so we never give the devil a foothold.

I. The State of Restoration
'I will restore the fortunes of my people Israel, and they shall rebuild the ruined cities and inhabit them;
they shall plant vineyards and drink their wine, and they shall make gardens and eat their fruit.' - Amos 9:4

The biblical meaning of restoration is to receive back more than has been lost. This is when our final state is greater than our original condition or when we have been improved beyond measure and our shame has dissolved away bringing with it our healing. That sounds like a really good deal, doesn't it? Yet what would you say if told that this good deal is totally in our hands, and all the wonderful things mentioned above cannot happen if we do not acquiesce to certain things first? In our pursuit of God's forgiveness, we have cried out to Him with a contrite and humble heart, we have fasted and prayed, staring our sins in the face and eschewing them. We surrendered our all to Him by confessing and repenting of these sins even as we forgave ourselves. Then we tapped into the mercies of Him who provides and forgives. God has renewed our mindsets and now we are restored. You see, restoration happens only after we go through the repentance process. 'And after you have suffered a little while, the God of all grace, who has called you to His eternal glory in Christ, will Himself restore, confirm, strengthen and establish you.' – 1Peter 5:10 This verse explains it all. He Himself will restore us, confirm, strengthen and establish us to His eternal glory in Christ. God no longer holds our sins to our account because 'as far as the east is from the west, so far has He removed our transgression from us.' – Psalm 103:12 But how does all this come together? The state of our restoration is by the power of the Holy Spirit. To all who believe in Jesus Christ's work on the cross, God pours out His Spirit. Joel describes in His prophecy in Joel 2:28, that God will pour out His Spirit upon all flesh. All flesh! Yes, the Holy Spirit is an agent of life and restoration to all.

The father in our parable described his younger son saying 'this brother of yours was dead, but is alive again.' – Luke 15:32 Restoration is when spiritual death is replaced by spiritual life. We can identify with the prodigal son; we were wayward, depraved, wicked and dead, but God, through the power of the Spirit sought us out and caused us to 'come to our senses' then He restored us. He improved our quality of life, made up for all our losses and gave us more than we previously had. What manner of love is this? It is always God's desire to make us whole again. The state of restoration calls for faith. Ephesians 2:8-9 says 'For it is by grace you have been saved, through faith – and this is not from yourselves, it is the gift of God - not by works, so that no one can boast.' It took faith for the prodigal son to turn his life around. As a young boy, the prodigal son may have studied scripture many times with his older brother under the tutelage of their father, who taught them about faith and salvation. The father probably taught his sons that without faith it is impossible to please God, Hebrews 11:6. He may have reminded them that God's grace was what worked their salvation and it took just faith for this gift to be received. And that gift was Christ offered on the cross. The prodigal son might have recalled a verse his father had made him memorize as a child, 'I have come that they may have life and have it more abundantly.' – John 10:10, 'An abundant life?' He said to himself now. Had he not squandered his quota of abundance? Could there be something else? After his waywardness? Was that still possible in this distant country where pig food was the order of the day? These scriptures must have propelled his dormant faith into action, and caused the events that brought him full circle. It is all about my Father, he said to himself. He has restored me. This son thus got a triple portion of restoration that day when he came to his senses. He had forgiven himself, been forgiven by God and his faith had been restored. How great is our Lord!

The state of restoration is also a time of prayer. That sense of freedom and joy cannot be taken for granted, for the abundance of grace always calls for more prayer. Restoration is truly a time of worship and thanksgiving. What God has done for us must be shouted from the roof-tops, we dare not rest on our laurels. The devil wants us to stay unforgiven forever so he is never pleased when we accept the call for repentance. Therefore, we must take time to pray as never before, thanking God for His great mercies and asking for grace to carry on in life. It is also a good time to pray for the unforgiven, that they also may receive this special gift. Perhaps the father of the prodigal son knew this full well. He had been forgiven and restored so he knew his job had been cut out for him. He prayed fervently to receive even more restoration by his wayward son's return. As he prayed on that lonely roof-top, along came his son. Oh, what a joy. Indeed, the state of restoration always brings us more.

II. The Heart of God
"'At that time I will gather you; at that time, I will bring you home. I will give you honor and praise among all the people of the earth when I restore your fortunes before your very eyes" says the Lord.' - Zephaniah 3:20

God has a heart for restoration which He portrays in many ways. Israel had provoked and sinned against God once again, but He called them to repentance and restored the remnant again. Time and again, we disobey God but He calls us out to Him, restores us and creates a right relationship with Him. It does not matter how deep the iniquity, He wants to bring us back into that right relationship so we can be filled with joy and contentment as we fellowship with Him. God is our fiercest advocate and provider. He wears His heart on His sleeve where His children are concerned. He will never leave us nor forsake us and He never gives up on us. The minor prophet Zephaniah in his prophecy declares beautifully the actions one must take when restoration has been bestowed upon us. In the third chapter of his book, we appreciate the work of restoration that God gives to His people, and the reaction it should emit from us. Verse 14 of chapter three says there should be singing, loud shouting, gladness and rejoicing in all our hearts! Why? For the Lord has taken away our judgments and turned back the enemy so there is nothing to fear and no harm ahead. In the verse 16, we are told to fear not nor let our hands hang limp. We pick up our spirits and lift up our hands in surrender, in praise, in prayer and in victory because God is mighty to save. He takes great delight in us and will no longer rebuke us. In the verses 18 and 19, we are reminded of special blessings that come our way when we have mourned our losses and we are assured of God's promise to deal with all who oppressed us and hindered our purposes. Finally, in the verse 20, it says 'at that time I will gather you; at that time, I will bring you home. I will give you honor and praise among all the peoples of the earth when I restore your fortunes before your very eyes.' What a declaration this is! This surely is the dance of restoration and speaks of God's strong love for us and the ever-present background work He does to ensure that we get to this restoration point if, and only if we choose to rend our hearts, repent, turn from our sins and accept the call of Jesus Christ.

God also demonstrates His heart for restoration through Grace. Grace is a fundamental part of God's character because it is His unconditional love poured on us – the undeserving. Since grace is the avenue by which God expresses His heart towards you and I, He is able to see beyond our transgressions and restore us back into His fold every day. Grace is favor, grace is love. 'For it is by grace you have been saved, through faith – and this is not from yourselves, it is a gift of God – not by works, so that no one can boast.' – Ephesians 2:8 This verse tells us that our restoration back to God is pure grace as long as we have faith to believe and accept that. 2Corinthians 5:21 also mentions how 'God made Him who had no sin to be sin for us, so that in Him we might become the righteousness of God.' We receive our forgiveness and restoration according to this grace that brings salvation to all men and it is this same grace that teaches us to live peaceful and harmonious lives. 2Peter 2:18 says 'we grow in the grace and knowledge of our Lord and Savior Jesus Christ.' Every single day, we must appreciate God's grace and give Him praise for it. As we stand in awe of His heart of love and abundant grace, God quickly forgives us, heals us and then restores us.

Finally, God's heart for restoration is beautifully revealed in our parable. In Luke 15:22,24 we read, 'But the father said to his servants, Quick! Bring the best robe and put it on him. Put a ring on his finger and sandals on his feet. Bring the fattened calf and kill it. Let's celebrate. For this son of mine was dead and is alive again; he was lost and is found.' So they began to celebrate.' The prodigal son had gone through the process of pursuing forgiveness, and was in his final course to face his father for restoration. Father on the other hand, had done the background work it took to reconcile and restore his son. When the younger son did the requisite confession and repentance, father provided the forgiveness and restoration. The new robe was the best in town, the ring was of fine quality and his new sandals must have cost a fortune, for 'this son of mine was dead and is alive again.' He regained his self-worth and the celebrations were already proceeding. This is what God has in store for each and every one of His beloved. Isaiah 57:17-19 sums up the state of God's heart in restoration after repentance. 'I was enraged by their sinful greed; I punished them, and hid My face in anger, yet they kept on in their willful ways. I have seen their ways, but I will heal them; I will guide them and restore comfort to Israel's mourners, creating praise on their lips. Peace, peace, to those far and near, says the Lord. "And I will heal them."' May the grace of our Lord Jesus Christ, the love of God, and the fellowship of the Holy Spirit, be with us now and always.

III. Pressed down, shaken together and running over
'Forgive and you will be forgiven: Give and it will be given to you. Good measure, pressed down, shaken together, running over, will be put in your lap. For with the measure you use it will be measured back to you.' - Luke 6:37b-38

By now, you may think you have been 'listening' to a broken record when I say God is all about loving relationships. I cannot say it enough. We can only shake our heads in utter amazement, when we try to decipher the extent of God's feelings for us all. It is a mystery that He alone in His sovereignty understands, and we are blessed to be on the receiving end of this wonder. The above verses highlight what happens after we repent of our sins, present them to the cross and forgive our offenders. God immediately allows us to obtain the forgiveness which He has already made available! It is like a dam waiting to burst its banks, or a parent watching a young child perform with bated breath. As soon as the banks give way, or the child's performance comes to a successful conclusion, there is pandemonium. The gushing of the water or the effusive celebration of the parent. So is this love that God has for us when we have, against all odds pursued forgiveness and have been drawn in. When God recompenses, He does so abundantly and even cause the angels to celebrate wildly. We do have a merciful God who blesses immensely when we turn back and come to Him. He showed this side of Himself when He forgave us by sending His son Jesus to die on the cross at Calvary so that our sins will be obliterated. All He asks is for us to acknowledge this, be remorseful over our own sins and forgive our offenders too. It is the law of reciprocity of sorts. It says 'for the measure you use it will be used to you.' You get what you reap, but in God's case, He improves our lot beyond the measure that we give. Not only do we receive something back, but restoration ensures that what we receive is much more.

Another example of God's multiplication when He restores can be found in Joel 2:25-26. He says 'I will repay you for the years the locusts have eaten – the great locust and the young locust, the other locusts and the locust swarm – my great army that I sent among you. You will have plenty to eat, until you are full, and you will praise the Name of the Lord your God, who has worked wonders for you; never again will my people be shamed.' Just imagine that! After the strong warnings of what can happen when one turns from God, the prophet Joel urges the people to fast and repent so that God will multiply and restore the total destruction of their harvest and bring years of abundance and favor.

Restoration is truly a great state of abundance that is available to all. The prodigal son moved from that state of severe famine with only pig pods available for food to a fattened calf served by his own father's servants. The father also moved from a state where 'this brother of yours was dead, but is alive again, was lost but now found.' – Luke 15:32 The angels join us to celebrate our abundance that come with restoration. Let us resolve in our hearts dear friend, that our pursuit of God's forgiveness will not be in vain. It should not be a half-hearted effort. We have to work at it in such a way that we reap God's abundance, pressed down, shaken together and running over. Let us purpose in our hearts to give our lives back to God in Christ and allow God to change affairs within us, like our prodigal son did and like his father did, because it leads to praise, precipitated by pardon and then bountiful provision. For it is only when we experience God's forgiveness that we can live a restored life.

IV. A Joyful Noise
'Shout for joy to God, all the earth! Sing the glory of His name; make His praise glorious.' - Psalm 66:1-2

We make a joyful noise when God does marvelously in our lives. In this chapter, we have established that pursuing God's forgiveness is the most significant undertaking in our lives for 'all have sinned and fall short of the glory of God.' – Romans 3:23 We discussed being contrite over our sins, our need to fast, repent and submit in humility. We followed the progress of the prodigal son and saw him make some dramatic strides in his transition from a harassed wanderer kinsman to a forgiven person. The angels rejoiced mightily when this heart change was detected, and restoration took place.

In the parable trilogy in Luke 15, of which we are considering the third – the Lost Son, Jesus responds to the Pharisees and the teachers of the law who were outraged that He associated with sinners. Jesus taught them that God's interest was in the salvation of every lost soul. In the first of the trilogy, when the lost sheep was found, there was great joy and celebration in Heaven. In like manner, when the woman in the second parable of the trilogy found her lost coin, she called her friends and neighbors and threw a big party and again, Heaven did not forget her joy. In the final parable of the trilogy, the Lost Son, there are several instances of joyful noises. I believe the younger son could not stop crying and shouting for joy when it dawned on him that he could truly go back home. He was beside himself with gladness when he realized that the chains had been broken and he was a forgiven person. His father, on the other side, could also not stop the loud burst of joyful song as he run across the field towards his son. Totally oblivious to what some may have thought of him, he kept his eyes only on his boy, because he felt the goodness of God in his heart. At the final embrace in the fields for all to see, father and son shared a joyful song. This song was probably based on Psalm 100 and with father's baritone and the prodigal's softer tenor, they must have burst out loudly in unison 'Shout for joy to the Lord, all the earth. Worship the Lord with gladness; come before Him with joyful songs. Know that the Lord is God. It is He who made us, and we are His; we are His people, the sheep of His pasture. Enter His gates with thanksgiving and His courts with praise; give thanks to Him and praise His name. For the Lord is good and His love endures forever; His faithfulness continues through all generations. Arm in arm, this father supported his son's emaciated structure, as they walked into the home where the real celebrations were fast beginning.

I often wonder what kind of music and dancing the older brother in the parable of the lost son actually heard coming from inside the home. Luke 15:25 says 'Meanwhile the older son was in the field. When he came near the house, he heard music and dancing.' A show had been put on and there was indeed a joyful noise. The father had planned this day for a long time, and the willing neighbors did not disappoint him. The music was thunderous, the dancing in high motion, the fattened calf was making its way to the banquet table and there was much rejoicing. But the question still remains. What did the older son hear? What songs did the angels sing? What music were they making? What were the celebrants dancing to? I am inclined to believe that it was all about praise and worship in that house. 'Worthy are you Oh Lord, mighty in power, holy and majestic!' On and on with the music, coupled with tambourines and stringed instruments. Friend, there is great joy when God forgives. Shout for joy and let the world know. It is also incumbent to mention that God's restoration produces gratitude and confidence in us. Since meeting Jesus, and joining ourselves to Him in faith, gratitude naturally springs up in our hearts towards God. We cannot help but consider our narrow escape from certain death to abundant life. Gratitude calls for God-glorification. No more self-glorification which was our old way, but glorifying God from a new joyful place in our hearts. As we appreciate our forgiven state, we share it confidently. How can we just not share our joyful gratitude when we feel specially forgiven? A joyful noise surely makes us able to pay it forward.

Finally, in the joy of our restoration, we yearn to make amends. We do not know for sure if the younger son would pay back the inheritance he took from his father, but what we know is that he was prepared to work with the servants and leave his life of privilege. He sure was not bitter about that, just grateful for life and forgiveness. When we consider Zacchaeus up in the sycamore tree, awed by Christ's love, his repentance was instant, and he was ready to seek forgiveness and make amends. In Luke 19:8, 'Zacchaeus stood up and said to the Lord, 'Look, Lord! Here and now I give half of my possessions to the poor and if I have cheated anybody out of anything I will pay back four times the amount.' Dear God, thank You for teaching us about our need to doggedly pursue the forgiveness that You lovingly provided by dying on the cross. Thank You for prompting us to repent of our sins so we are restored to You for eternity. Thank You for the blessings that come with restoration; massive joy, overwhelming abundance, freedom and peace. We are also thankful that now, we cannot bear to hold any grudge in our hearts against our offenders, because we cannot see past Your loving grace. So here we are, as we are, awesomely forgiven, we will pay it forward and be called forgivers. Help us to stand ready to enfold our offenders.

PART C
STAND READY TO ENFOLD

We learned in the previous section that God has loved us deeply from the very beginning and continues to do so and this will never change. We learned also that His desire to forgive us was adequately demonstrated by the events on the cross. This too will never change. He extends forgiveness for sins, and He expects us to reach up in repentance to receive it always. We are the problem unfortunately. We do not allow Him to take those sins and grudges and pin them to Jesus on the cross so that the forgiveness transaction can be wonderfully completed and result in reconciliation and restoration. Ultimately, all un-repented sinners cannot inherit the kingdom of God, not because God did not love them, but because they never went in pursuit of God's forgiveness.

The following scripture, illustrates our point adequately. Nehemiah 9:16-17 (KJV) 'But they and our fathers dealt proudly, and hardened their necks, and hearkened not to thy commandments, and refused to obey, neither were mindful of thy wonders that thou didst among them; but hardened their necks, and in their rebellion appointed a captain to return to their bondage: but thou art a God ready to pardon, gracious and merciful, slow to anger, and of great kindness, and forsookest them not.' God's people always bring judgment upon themselves by being stiff necked and rebellious, but we know that He provides absolute forgiveness and stands ready to pardon because Christ died on the cross for our sins. This indicates that there is nothing that keeps God from pardoning us except when we refuse to receive it through Jesus Christ. God stands ready to pardon, if we are ready to accept it. He unequivocally wants us all to be saved, and so shall we be when we ask for this already provided forgiveness. He happily removes our stains and blemishes and showers His forgiveness on us. If we do not go to Heaven, we cannot blame God. He is stable - He is the forgiveness pillar. We must endeavor to anchor ourselves to this stable pillar by asking Him through confession and repentance to forgive us and take away all our sins.

I have frequently wondered about schools of thought that speak of the needlessness of human forgiveness when there is no requisite repentance and confession from an offender. The following Bible verse is often used to make that claim. Luke 17:3-4. This scripture says 'So watch yourselves. If your brother or sister sins against you, rebuke them; and if they repent, forgive them. Even if they sin against you seven times in a day and seven times come back to you saying "I repent", you must forgive them.' These schools of thought suggest that if our offender does not come to us in repentance, we do not have to forgive them. They argue that there are people who in due course will not inherit God's kingdom because they never repented of their sins, justifying the above verse. This is correct to a point, but one thing that is missed from this way of thinking however is that, God has done the entire forgiving work before we sinned against our brother or sister, so the fact that we do not rise up in repentance to meet His forgiveness does not mean it has not been extended. This process is what I like to call Standing Ready to enfold. Jesus in the Luke 17 passage indicated above, said these words to teach and encourage forgiveness with reconciliation. When we consider Jesus' words in Matthew 18, The ultimate hope and goal whenever there are rifts between neighbors is forgiveness that leads the way towards reconciliation. Hence to stop short at the need to attempt forgiveness because the obligatory repentance has not come would be detrimental to the victim. In a perfect world, this scenario is ideal, because both parties are already heading towards forgiveness with reconciliation. The forgiver seeks out the offender to admonish them about their faults and resolve issues, while the offender seeks out the victim to repent. The latter receives their forgiveness and both parties are joyfully reconciled. Reconciliation, being the ultimate goal of forgiveness, would be our greatest aspiration and this is what Jesus would want to see happen in all situations so that perfect peace and freedom can reign. It is all about loving relationships! It is therefore mind-boggling that one would think to stop short of forgiveness because they assume that the process must always end at the doorstep of reconciliation. And because reconciliation is not always the case, they would rather just not offer to forgive an offender at all if he does not come back in repentance. This would mean that the victim will hold on to the grudge and pain without letting it go. If that were the case, Bible verses that also say that we must forgive our offenders just as Christ forgave us would be redundant. Ephesians 4:32 says 'Be kind and compassionate to one another, forgiving each other, just as in Christ God forgave you.' And the Bible verse in Romans 12:18 that admonishes us that if possible, and as long as it depends on us to live in peace with each other, would also be unnecessary.

Our new topic, Stand Ready to enfold, tries to refute these claims and encourage forgiveness with or without reconciliation. If the relationship will not end in reconciliation, we still must forgive our offender. We now want to build on this foundation by establishing that once we have pursued God's forgiveness and received it, we have to pay it forward. We always hope we can forgive and reconcile as advocated by

Jesus in Luke 17:3, and yet we have to ensure that we have extended forgiven in our hearts no matter the circumstances. God forgave us in His heart prior to our sinful events, and we must do likewise. Colossians 3:13 says 'Bear with each other and forgive one another if any of you have a grievance against someone. Forgive as the Lord forgave you.' Endeavor, dear friend to take the path of forgiveness toward reconciliation. If the offender does not meet us on the other side of the path in repentance, we know that we have released the debt to God and 'forgiven just as the Lord forgave' and our heart is void of the weight of the grudge.

CHAPTER NINE
WITH ALL OUR HEARTS

The onset of forgiveness means that our hearts have been wounded from a sin done against us. It is our Christian duty to heal the wounded heart by way of releasing the bitter pain to the cross of Jesus. Whenever we contemplate forgiveness, we are admonished to take a good look at our hearts and decide to humbly set the forgiveness ball rolling because of all the benefits that come with it. Of course we cannot start the forgiveness process by ourselves. We need the Holy Spirit to engulf our hearts with compassion and give us the needed strength to find a way to forgive. We are then empowered to make that bold decision to let go of all the grudges within. When we stop to think about it though, all forgiveness is really a matter of self-forgiveness, or heart forgiveness, so when we do forgive, we are actually forgiving our negative judgments of another person's actions. We are also letting go of ego so we can forgive our condemnation of them. C.S. Lewis[13] says 'To be a Christian means to forgive the inexcusable, because God has forgiven the inexcusable in you'

I. An attitude of Forgiveness
'Forgiveness is not an occasional act. It is a permanent attitude.'
-Martin Luther King Jr. [14]

Standing ready to enfold reminds us of another parable Jesus told in Matthew 18:26-27 where the unmerciful servant, begged for and received mercy for his debt but refused to forgive a smaller debt from a fellow servant. He did not apply the important scripture that admonishes us to forgive just as we have been forgiven. Alas, his reservation to Heaven was denied him and he was handed over to his tormentors. This story is poignant, because it teaches us profoundly to stand ready to enfold our debtors at all times. How do we do this? Well, the concept of forgiveness has had a challenging portrayal from time immemorial, so it is essential that we understand the practical ways of standing ready to enfold very simply and distinctly in order that it becomes an effortless habit. Many resist the idea of forgiving an offender because they believe the offender may be getting off easy, going scot-free while they suffer unfairly from the consequences of the offender's actions. On occasion, some may think forgiveness must lead to reconciliation, so they would rather not attempt forgiveness at all since they do not want to be 'friendly' with the person who hurt them so badly. It is detrimental to our own salvation when we refuse to consider forgiveness for the reasons stated above. 'Today,' the Bible says in Hebrews 3:15, 'if you hear His voice, do not harden your heart as you did in rebellion.' We discussed earlier that God has granted our forgiveness on the cross at Calvary, and it is up to us to rise up in repentance to receive it. In our first chapter, we defined forgiveness as 'to give ahead of the crime.' We emulate God's example of forgiveness, because we have received forgiveness from Him so we work towards that release of our offenders too – that is the 'as' in Colossians 3:13, 'forgive as the Lord forgave you.' That is 'as' God does, we do too! Ahead of time, readily, willingly and quickly, we release the sin to Him, then He does the washing away.

What then am I saying? God's forgiveness is one by which He frees sinners from judgment, and delivers them from the penalties of sin. This, as stated many times already, is done through the shed blood of His son Jesus Christ, who wipes away all sins, and makes us righteous in His own sight. Indeed,

God's forgiveness is all encompassing because in His sovereignty, He is able to use that blood to scoop us from the horror of sin and change our status so we can be Heaven ready. Likewise, we are mandated to forgive our offenders by separating them from their sins and lifting the hateful offenses up to God while resuming a loving relationship − where possible − with them. From both a spiritual and human perspective, the blueprint for the process of forgiveness seems the same because both involve a sinner being released from their sins − but there is a big difference in the result of this separation process. The difference between divine and human forgiveness is that we forgive internally, from our hearts, by deciding to separate the sin from the offender and presenting it to God. He then sees the sin that has been presented to Him on the cross and expunges it fully. It will always be a continuum for us; but thanks be to God, because 'it is finished' with the Lord! John 19:30. This is why our power to forgive always needs the God-touch to be fully accomplished. We can therefore forgive everyone, even those who have not acknowledged their wrongs, nor shown contrition, because it is an inner heart event on our part which God completes perfectly for us. That is also why we extend forgiveness contentedly, knowing that this utmost human virtue will always reveal God's loving character, exemplified on the cross! Friend, let us train our hearts to embrace the virtue of forgiveness with all our might, remembering that this transaction is always to test our genuine commitment to God. Indeed, granting forgiveness, will always be a blow to our pride, it will always go against the sentiments of the flesh, thus making its accomplishment the height of humility and the very portrayal of love.

As far as it depends on us therefore, we have to make it easy for our offenders to approach us when they are ready to seek our forgiveness. We should not avoid them, if their intentions to repent have been made clear to us. In standing ready to enfold we can also seek them out and forgive them verbally as the Holy Spirit prompts us. Bible says for God so loved the world, that He gave His son. God was standing ready long before we confessed our sins. Do permit me to sound more like a broken record dear reader, for these points are very essential. Sins against us may be intense, brutal, puke-evoking and almost unforgivable, but think about the plight of God. He is hit with sin from all angles, every minute of the day, yet still, He forgives and stands ready to reconcile and restore. Though He suffered more, not only does He forgive, He is ready and able to wash away our sins and then cleanse the effects of the sin. In the perfect scenario, we would wait till all our ducks are in a row, our rebukes and confrontations have yielded humility, the offender's heart has softened and 'kumbaya' has taken place. But unfortunately not, we know that real life situations are always complicated. The offender has moved on or away, he or she does not have the humility to repent, does not consider their actions towards us as sinful, may be spiritually unavailable for reprove or we cannot rebuke them for a reason or other so, do we have to hold on until the situation is perfect? No. We immediately yearn in our hearts through prayer, to develop an absolute forgiving attitude always, with no rebellious thoughts, no resistance, no weigh-ins, just forgiveness. It is our Christian obligation to pardon our offenders faithfully, and by grace we can do so. Ephesians 4:32 says 'Be kind and compassionate to one another, forgiving each other, just as in Christ, God forgave you.' If the offense done against us was unimaginably dreadful and has caused too much anger, pain and suffering, am I suggesting that even so we must forgive? Unequivocally I am, friend, yes, I am! We have to find a way to quit gritting our molars over the pain and intensity of atrocious sins against us. Instead, we must grit our molars in the wonder of becoming forgiven beings.

Friend, we have looked at the need to forgive just as God forgave us several times now, so let us go ahead and forgive with all our hearts. With the Holy Spirit on our side, we can do this. We will not justify the reasons why the grudge continues to be lodged in our hearts. We will shake it away and let it go. We will not always wait for our offender to repent. Regardless, we still have to forgive because it is all about God's grace on our lives and not the enormity of their sin. We will keep in mind that God does the work of completing the forgiveness process in our hearts. God's forgiveness becomes an incentive for us to forgive our offenders. But if the sinner does repent, that is great because we will be well on our way towards reconciliation. If unable to rebuke him on the matter as suggested in our introduction above, Luke 17:3, we sure will go ahead and release the venom from our hearts and pass our offender's sins to Christ on the cross and leave them there. That is how it is done.

II. On the Look-Out
'Forgiveness is the fragrance that the violet sheds on the heel that has crushed it.' -Mark Twain15

Is there anyone in your life that you have to forgive? There is no statute of limitation on granting forgiveness so if there is such a person, get on with forgiving them now. Many of us have pushed the need to forgive an offender so far back into our hearts that we seem to have forgotten to do so. Maybe, we waited for an apology that never came. Maybe we did not know the importance of releasing the debt of sin ahead of time, so we have been sitting around with the hurt for so long. The act of forgiveness has been taken for granted for too long, so it's about time we step up and begin some serious forgiving of our own. We know that if we do not forgive our offender, God will not forgive us for our sins as well. We also know that if we do not repent of our own sins, God's forgiveness though granted to us remains unclaimed. Now is the time to seek out everyone who has offended us or who we have offended and begin rectifying every situation. I chose 'On the look-out' for this portion of the book to embolden us to get on the forgiveness band wagon and do so with all we have. Being on the look-out means living our lives with the work of the cross ever before us. Looking at Jesus crucified makes it much easier to bestow forgiveness. There is this quote from the author Alan Paton[16] which says, 'When a deep injury is done to us, we never recover until we forgive.' Our frames were truly not made to carry resentment and grudges. Much as we hurt or are angry at the person who caused the pain, we have to do all we can to rid our hearts of the grudge, so we can move on with our lives. It has been suggested that forgiveness requires the strongest love contained in the human soul, and to that I add, we can find that love in Christ Jesus, always. How best can we be challenged to forgive our offenders? What if they never step up to the plate and repent? What if they were strangers so there is no chance of us ever finding them again? What if we cannot even remember who we have offended or who has offended us in the past? The answer to all these questions is to be on the look-out as we stand ready to restore relationships. Mark 13:33 says 'Be on your guard! Be alert! You do not know when that time will come.'

The father in our parable stood on his roof-top and looked out for the chance to complete the forgiveness transaction. He had played the initial and crucial part in his heart already by releasing his son's debt of sin to the cross. Now when he reconciles with his son, the entire transaction would be wondrously complete. From that vantage point, and with forgiveness foremost on his mind, father could survey and remember all who needed forgiveness and who he had to seek forgiveness from. Being on the look-out calls for heart alertness. This means a keen observation and watchfulness that happens within our hearts. God has enabled us to use our hearts to observe life. Bible says in Psalm 46:10b to 'be still and know that He is God.' When we keep still within our hearts, the Holy Spirit helps us recall personal grievances that have not been forgiven and prompts us to work on these issues. We have to be vigilant in this watch, for our lives depend on this. 1Peter 5:8 says 'Be alert and of sober mind. Your enemy the devil prowls around like a roaring lion looking for someone to devour.' Being on the look-out also means keeping our minds attentive and ready for action. The enemy uses the problem of unforgiveness to try sabotaging God's plans and our call to advance kingdom work and making it to Heaven. The subtle use of an unforgiving heart will cause many of us to be thrown to our tormentors. If we are not on the look-out then, the devil will cause us to forget those who need forgiveness in our lives and our hearts will be hardened against any form of forgiveness. Though he cannot steal our salvation from us, the devil can and does deceive. He has not changed his deceptive ways. By being sober-minded, the devil does not stand a chance because we are always on the look-out. We stare into the horizon of our lives, ever ready to pounce on the chance at forgiving everyone for everything. We move on from being bitter and holding on to grudges, for we remember with joy all that God forgave us for. 2Corinthians 10:5 helps us to arrest every unforgiving action and give it to Christ. 'We demolish arguments and every pretension that sets itself up against the knowledge of God, and we take captive every thought and make it obedient to Christ.'

Friend, since being on the look-out calls for vigilance and determination, we must endeavor to forgive at every opportunity. 1Thessalonians 5:6 says 'So then, let us not be like others, who are asleep, but let us be awake and sober.' Forgive the big things and the little things as we have them listed in our hearts and minds. We must focus all our attention on finding ways and means to forgive everything as the Holy Spirit counsels us. Our decision to do so will help us not to focus so much on the sin itself, but focus on how to clear our hearts and if possible, win the sinner back. Remember that a full-scale reconciliation is not what is being discussed here, though that is always God's will for us, but rather, the need to be intent on letting go of bitterness that the wrong done to us brought about. The father in our story spent countless hours up on his roof-top, looking out for his son. Let the world be surprised that we want to forgive our offender so badly. May they wonder why we yearn to do so. It may be an opportunity to share our love for God with others. Society condones the right to bear an unforgiving heart and this is not God's way. When we conform to societal standards where forgiveness is concerned, it will be our downfall. We have been called to 'forgive as God forgave.' May we be faithful and wise to listen, and may God help us apply a heart of forgiveness always. Let us be on the look-out to forgive everything. It is so worth it.

III. A time of Intercession
'And pray in the Spirit on all occasions with all kinds of prayers and requests. With this in mind, be alert and always keep on praying for all the Lord's people.' - Ephesians 6:18

Perhaps here is one of the more difficult portions of this work. We are called to intercede for those who persecute us. It says in Matthew 5:44 'But I tell you, love your enemies and pray for those who persecute you.' Intercession is the will of God and sometimes confusing as it may sound, our words of intercession for our offender is what God will base His method of justice on. Our intercession for our offenders is a form of humility. We tell God that we are depending on Him to take the pain of the sin away, and do with it as He pleases. 1Timothy 2:1 says 'I urge, then, first of all, that petition prayers, intercession and thanksgiving be made for all people.' The verse three says 'this is good and pleases God our Savior who wants all people to come to a knowledge of the truth.' As this verse suggests, God wants everyone to be saved, and our intercession for the person who has hurt us allows God to work on the heart of the offender. Interestingly, God can decree that the prayers of some people will be received for the guilt of others. A good example is from Job 42:7-8 where God is angry at the three friends of Job, and will only accept prayers from Job on their behalf. This tells us how important intercessory prayers are. God in His wisdom mandates this, and whether it is to speed up the restoration process, cause reconciliation or forgiveness, we do not know. Let us approach God and talk to Him on behalf of our offenders. We have to be diligent in praying for those who have hurt us because we may be the appointed means by which someone escapes the consequences of their folly.

Do you remember how Jesus said in Luke 23:34 'Father forgive them, for they do not know what they are doing?' In His agony, Jesus knew that His tormentors did not know the effect of their sin on their own lives. They may have just been doing their jobs or they could also have been truly happy inflicting pain on Jesus, but that is not the point under discussion. The fact is, God still loved them too and wanted them to repent and be saved. Stephen did the same thing in Acts 7:60 when he said 'Lord, do not hold this sin against them.' This was when he was being stoned to death for what his persecutors thought was him blaspheming. Again, in his agony, he interceded on their behalf. What is common to both instances is that they looked up steadfastly to God because that was where their heart was. They trusted God completely to take care of their pain. With our eyes on the Lord, we too will be beyond the pain being inflicted on us. Jesus and Stephen were living their lives and enduring their deaths only to please God, and so must we too. We have to yearn to look up to God unwaveringly when we are in agony of any kind. Let us not worry about how God will take care of our offenders. We must rest assured that He will take care of our hurting situation in the best possible way. Leave it to Him.

Sometimes, our offenders are not repentant because they do not feel that they have sinned against us, or they may not know how to go about expressing remorse. Will we snub them, or take them seriously? Our offenders may also have acted in ignorance, immaturity or on a foolish impulse. As we intercede, God works on both hearts, and the rebuking and repenting process discussed above in Luke 17, will occur beautifully. Though it should never be our goal to wish ill on our offenders, interceding for them is the best way to get the needed justice meted out to them. Our intercessory prayers for these people must never be because we want them to suffer or come running to grovel at our feet. These prayers are not to meet any selfish need or cause the sinner to live up to our expectations. We do not use intercessory prayers to obtain an apology, but that God's will be done. Such prayers must be motivated by love. We already discussed that our God is a just God, so He knows exactly what to do with the sin that has been presented to Him as we separate it from the offender.

In our intercessory prayers therefore, we have to learn to separate the painful sin from the sinner. We must hand over the sin to God, and enfold the sinner for restoration's sake. Mark 11:25 reminds us that if we hold anything against anyone, we have to forgive them so that God in Heaven will forgive us. This is not impossible if we seek God steadfastly and allow the Holy Spirit to assist us. Friend, let us gaze intently at God as we intercede for our offenders. He will empower us, and soften our hearts and help us to succeed in extending forgiveness.

IV. A Father's Prayer
'My child, your sins are forgiven,' – Mark 2:5b

Early each morning, when father in our Luke 15 parable of the Lost Son woke up, he would go up and take his seat on his roof-top and begin to pray. His prayers were simple:
'Heavenly Father, I bow to you today, King of kings, to magnify You. I exalt You because of Your love that knows no limits. Thank You for Your grace unmeasurable, and the gift of

unconditional forgiveness, provided on the Calvary cross. I am forever grateful. Thank You for allowing me to draw close to You to repent and confess my own sins, and the grace to extend that same forgiveness. Give me the strength to never have any ill-will against my prodigal son and my older son. I need Your strength to continue to be free of all anger, bitterness and unforgiveness. Fill me with the power of Your Spirit to be empowered to do Your will.'

Day in and day out, hour after hour, father would repeat similar prayer to God as he continued vigil on his roof-top. Sometimes this father would complement prayers for his family with a fast. He was particularly prayerful about the sibling rivalry between his two sons. He himself regretted not paying much attention in the past few years, but he had prayed for forgiveness on that score. Now, he lifted his children before the Lord, praying that they lived uprightly, honoring God and each other. He prayed that he would learn to calm their turbulent relationship while showing no signs of favoritism, and portray the love of Christ to them. He prayed that his faith would continue to be strengthened and his confidence always boosted. He believed that the incident with his younger son was just what was needed to draw his child back to God, so he was determined to see it in that light since he believed it to be the right thing. His only hope was that God would protect his son in his period of edification. He wanted his son to rededicate his life to Christ and come back home. His son's brash, direct and confident way of approaching life could be put to good use as an agent of God's Kingdom, he mused. The father also remembered that he had not done such a good job with his older son. The father-son time together they previously enjoyed had diminished altogether. He knew his older son was still angry with him for doing the younger's bidding, but he felt he had no choice at the time. God help him, this father prayed. He was determined to teach forgiveness to both his sons.

Father stood up from his praying position and begun to scan the horizon. No minute detail eluded him. He saw everything, and for some reason, he even believed his eye sight was improving since starting this vigil. Thank God for extended prayers he thought. Sometimes, he said to himself, severe trials can bring additional blessings. His health was actually improving, with all that fasting and prayer. With a wistful smile on his face, he turned his eyes back to the horizon. One thing this father knew for sure was that he was standing ready to enfold his prodigal son back into his arms and his life, just as God had done for him. Such was the love God had for him and so was his own love for his younger son. Deep was his desire to assure his son that all was well and he was ready to start over. Not once did father ponder negatively over the deep grief his son had caused him. He had forgiven his son a long time ago and was just intent on renewing their relationship. Once in a while, a niggling feeling would come over him that this problem could repeat itself once this immediate one was rectified, but he did not give much attention to that thought. He just said to himself, 'get thee behind me Satan, I have much to be thankful to God for, and He knows how to take care of me.' The father's main concern was that the outcome would be reconciliation, restoration and love. This reminds us of two things. First, the definition of the word 'forgive' which emphasizes the giving back love afore the crime. Secondly the verse in 1Corinthians 13 that says that 'love keeps no record of wrongs' was seared into his heart. This is deep, but totally achievable when we look to God's grace.

Dear friend, when we stand ready to enfold our offender, we wake up early, spend time in prayer and then begin to scan the horizon of our hearts. This is simply looking out for ways and opportunities to express to our offender that we no longer hold them responsible for the pain they caused. That is what forgiveness is and does. Scanning the horizon does not involve re-living the sin. Our vigil is not a time to replay what happened in a negative way, nor try to remember the details of the hurtful words. It is certainly not a time to be upset that we cannot recall the exact details and facts about the sin. When we stand ready to enfold, we think about words and phrases that can possibly gather the offender back into our arms. We do not worry about what he or she will do again once we enfold them. We focus on 1Peter 4:8 which says, 'Above all, love each other deeply, because love covers over a multitude of sins' We just let God worry about future consequences of our desire to enfold and love our offenders. God's wisdom will surely lead us into the right paths. When we stand ready to enfold, our prayers are thanksgiving prayers for our own forgiven state. In solitude, up on our roof-top, we pray fervently, rejoicing that God has brought us this far. We are grateful that our sins against God and man have been washed away by the blood of Jesus. We rejoice in that time of solitude, prior to reconciliation with our offender, that we too can forgive. The dear father, with his improving eyesight, made every effort to analyze every individual on the horizon, checking out their gait, wondering, hoping that this time it would be his younger son. He so yearned for such a reunion. From time to time, he would call down to the servants and ask if the fattened calf was in good condition. Such was his faith, and deep was his forgiveness.

As we think about forgiveness, the most important thing is to just do it. Let us go deep into our hearts and release our offenders and not worry about the repercussions. God knows of all possible repercussions and has plans for its circumvention. With that in mind, go ahead and forgive! Forgive the offender who might not even appreciate it! Remember, release is not synonymous to reconciliation. Our only work is taking the resentment out of us and giving it to God, so that when we regard this person, we are no longer hurt and we want to restore the relationship when possible. It can be done by the grace of God. If we have been forgiven of our own sins, then we too must go ahead and ask for grace to pardon unconditionally. God will grant this request for He sees our hearts and He is faithful.

CHAPTER 10
SPIRIT OF COMPASSION

Compassion is such a powerful tool in the Christian realm. To have compassion is to feel sympathy or to have mercy on another soul who is suffering. Some have described compassion as seeing through the eyes of God. It allows us to empathize with someone who is going through a difficult situation. When we do not feel compassion, we have declined to put ourselves in a person's position to understand their suffering. What does this have to do with forgiveness you may ask? Why should we feel compassion for someone who may have wounded us? Well, we yearn to be like Jesus and so by adopting components of compassion, which consists of perceiving the infraction or setback, desiring to do something about it and acting on it, we get better at forgiving our offenders. When we have been hurt, we feel so injured and angry that we sometimes refuse to see past our anger. We become victim, martyr, hero and champion and we sometimes use such circumstances to minimize our own sins against God and others. This is a subtle trick the devil uses to forge an unforgiving heart within us. Yet by using the components of compassion, we are forced to acknowledge the offender's point of view, and many times, if we peer deep enough, we will feel sorry for them. They may be ignorant, unwise, immature, and many other reasons for wanting to hurt us. It may also be willful on their part for which we should feel doubly sorry for them, because they do not know Christ, and this may be our perfect opportunity to be used to change that.

I. Components of Compassion
'So he got up and went to his father. But while he was still a long way off, his father saw him and was filled with

compassion for him; he ran to his son, threw his arms around him and kissed him.' - Luke 15:20

Father was suddenly feeling particularly jubilant. Up on his roof-top, a sudden lightness had taken over his soul when he realized that the puzzling tug he had been feeling in his heart all day was compassion for his son. Compassion is the key needed in fostering the ability to forgive others entirely. Once this father put himself in his younger son's shoes, it helped him understand or maybe appreciate why the boy had acted the way he did. Father did not approve of what occurred, but he certainly had grown to understand his son's mindset better. In the same way, friend, once we understand the why of the sin, we are compelled to forgive faster. This compassion and forgiveness relationship also help us to grow to be more like Jesus, who was able to forgive His offenders in the midst of His agony on the cross. Thus, a heart immersed in compassion will always take a positive action when it comes into contact with suffering. For compassion to work at its peak, there are key components that must always be recognized and applied. First on the compassion components list is the perception. We perceive the predicament of a person. We are alerted through our senses to this problem, then the acquired knowledge signals our desire to act. The desire to take action is the next key. Once the desire comes into our hearts, we act on it by making a move to sort out the predicament. The action is the final key of the component of compassion. Compassion has arrived. It appealed to our senses and we reacted positively to the situation. Compassion must always make its debut with gratitude. We look at God and feel grateful for His love for us and we always want to pass that on.

In looking at our father in our parable, we can understand the components of compassion better. In Luke 15:20 stated above, father saw his prodigal son from a distance, and was filled with compassion. He had applied the first component of compassion. The Holy Spirit allowed his senses to perceive his son's predicament. Next, the Spirit signaled him to react positively to the problem in sight, the desire had come and with that, he acted on the knowledge by running to meet his son. Compassion had come rushing into his heart and it compelled him to act positively. Bible said 'he ran to his son, threw his arms around him and kissed him.' Compassion always appeals to our senses, and causes a positive reaction. The father, who in today's world, will be viewed as the victim, felt the plight of his younger son, after seeing his son through God's eyes. He threw all decorum to wind when his fragile looking son came into his view, and run to embrace him, showing great affection that only compassion can do. Lamentations 3:22 says 'Because of the Lord's great love we are not consumed, for His compassions never fail.' Compassion must never fail once we adopt it. We cannot apply it one time and not apply it another time. It does not have a limit either so it must be something that we do at all times. Because of love, compassion is fail safe, and because of compassion, forgiveness is possible. We pray that God in His wisdom will help us to develop a compassionate spirit so that forgiveness can abound.

A companion of compassion which we cited above is gratitude. A grateful heart is when we are thankful to God for all we are and have. We cultivate a grateful heart as we become forgivers because we are constantly looking at our own salvation. Gratitude is the only proper response to God's grace so if we can always look past our trials and be grateful, there is nothing we cannot forgive. This is because God uses trials and temptations to make us stronger and help us to conform to the image of Christ. He equips us to endure our trials and tribulations for our own ultimate good and His great glory. We should therefore not be surprised when we see gratitude lingering where compassion dwells. As we think about our offender and the sins committed against us, the devastation gradually fades and we begin to feel a sense of gratitude that Jesus knows exactly what has happened and yet He still cares. We remember the verse that says 'all things work together for good to them that love the Lord.' – Romans 8:28 Gratitude spreads warmth in our hearts as we remember the many sins that God has already forgiven us, and this helps us to boldly show compassion and forgiveness towards our offender too.

God always looks on us with compassion and sympathy and that is exactly how we must begin to see our offender in the spirit of the enormity of the sin against us. When we lift them up before the Lord, He proceeds to remove not just their transgressions, but He reminds us that He does not hold our own sins against us anymore. Reader, we need to seriously develop what it takes to be compassionate and grateful. These are the means through which we can forgive others more easily as we submit the sins against us to God in obedience and trust.

II. Jesus, an example of Compassion
'For we do not have a high priest who is unable to empathize with our weaknesses, but we have one who has been tempted in every way, just as we are – yet He did not sin.' - Hebrews 4:15

Jesus is the compassionate gift to mankind. He came into the world to die for us so that all our sins could be forgiven. Without this great gift of love and compassion, there would be no hope for us at all. Our prayers would lack efficacy, there would be no reassurance in seeking God's forgiveness in confession and repentance, and the penalty of sin would never be removed. Thank God for Christ who is now exalted to God's right hand to intercede on our behalf so that when we repent of our sins, pardon follows quickly. Christ's compassion instructs us to be compassionate too because He can sympathize with all our feelings, our hurts, pain and trials. He pleads powerfully onto God to sustain, comfort and forgive us every day. If our great Advocate always works to ensure that we are cleansed by His blood, is not the least we can do to feel compassion for our offenders and show them Christ?

Let us take a look at how Jesus applied the components of compassion so we can employ the same qualities in our quest to becoming a forgiving people. In Mark 1:41, Jesus, 'moved with compassion, stretched out His hand and touched the man, "I am willing; be cleansed"' This was an incident where a leprous man begged for healing from Jesus. Jesus was moved, the Bible said. The perception came, He responded to the sick man, 'I am willing' to heal you. Desire followed perception closely and then action came. Jesus acted upon this in a positive manner and the man received his healing. Again, as is recorded in Luke 7:13, Jesus felt compassion for a widow who had just lost her only son. He saw her, the Bible said, and His heart reached out to her, and He acted positively by raising the son from the dead, based on the feelings elicited by compassion. Yet again, Jesus was filled with compassion for two blind men whom He proceeded to heal as is recorded in Matthew 20:34. He stopped, called out to them and touched them. There are several other instances in the bible where Jesus was filled with compassion and applied the components of compassion so that people in need, who had no ability to help themselves got the relief and joy they needed.

Christ's greatest show of compassion for humanity, bar none, was that He gave His life for us 'while we were still sinners.' – Romans 5:8 He perceived our need for a savior, He desired to be the means through which we would be reconciled to God, and He acted upon that by dying on the cross for you and I. The key components of compassion were applied by Jesus so that we would be fully reconciled to God. If we consider the extent of our sins that Christ Jesus forgave on the cross, we should also be filled with compassion for our offenders so that the sins done against us will be completely forgiven. As we also stand ready to enfold our offenders, we must imitate the example of our Savior's tender heart. We eschew the sins of our offenders just as we eschew our own sins. For when we understand the depth of our own sin and the enormity of God's mercy in forgiving us, we will freely forgive every evil committed against us. We are better able to see their sinful state when we allow compassion to wash over in our hearts. Then, the desire to forgive our offenders is easier. As to whether they repent and seek reconciliation, we know that our part has been played. God has been magnified.

III. On the Road to Jericho
'The expert in the law replied, "the one who had mercy on him."
Jesus told him, "Go and do likewise."' - Luke 10:37

In Luke 10:30-37, we read about a certain Samaritan who was journeying from Jerusalem to Jericho and came upon a man wounded by thieves and left for dead on the road. This Good Samaritan had compassion on the man when he saw his plight. He sympathized with him, and cared for him selflessly and at his own expense. He did not stop to think about the differences between the wounded man and himself, him being a Samaritan and the man a Jew. His compassion was not empty, not a quick glance or a prayer for his healing as the priest and Levite did earlier, but the Samaritan took steps to ensure that the wounded man received healing. He did all he could to ease the suffering of the man he did not even know. His compassion highlights God's kindness and love towards us. When we are robbed and stripped by the evil one or hurt beyond words by an offender, God sees us in our wretched and miserable state and has compassion on us. He cares for us at His own expense, shedding His blood that we might be saved.

Jesus demonstrates that we should 'go and do likewise' in Luke 10:37. What then can we give back to God in appreciation of such wonderful compassion and love? The Bible said to go and do likewise! What is 'likewise?' Likewise means we also show mercy at the drop of a hat, and not just any mercy, but the mercy that strikes us most – to our offenders. We must do so generously and with love. That is why it is our duty to be compassionate especially to our offenders. It is easy to be good to a good person, but there are more blessings in the effort we make towards our offenders. We piled on all our sins unto Jesus, but He never complained. Instead, He saw our sin from God's point of view which is amazing love. We too must be ready to forgive compassionately for it is particularly poignant since it takes amazing love and an extraordinary kind of grace to project. Compassion must overwhelm us and push us to react positively. Whether they know it or not, our offender is suffering under the weight of their sin. We must see our offender's sin for what it is – ugly, putrefying mess, just as God sees our sin. Then we must act quickly, just as the Samaritan did, just as the father in our parable story did and just as Jesus Christ always does for you and I. We must be ready to apply all the components of compassion with deep gratitude. We must perceive and be moved by our sinner's crime, desire to forgive them and then proceed to do so, releasing them from the debt of sin. My point is, we have to equate our sinner's sin to our own sin against God, and if we do want God to forgive us, then we do likewise. 'Go and do likewise, Luke 10:37'

IV. Compassion: Mark of a true Christian
'Therefore as God's chosen people, holy and dearly loved, clothe yourselves with compassion, kindness, humility, gentleness and patience.' - Colossians 3:12

We cannot be void of compassion and still call ourselves Christians. True compassion, as Christ practiced it, is an outpouring of deep mercy: 'clothe yourselves with compassion' says the above scripture. We are to wear compassion tenderly as true Christians. What a privilege to be considered holy and dearly loved by God and chosen to be a great example to others. Thus, when a person offends us greatly, we must pause and check our reaction. Can we take in a deep breath and apply the components of compassion – or are we so overly hurt and angry that we are completely blinded into a hardened heart? To be successful in forgiving our offender, it is important that we immediately bring the debts to Jesus, the author of compassion. The longer we bear our burden, pain and guilt, the more desolate and hopeless we feel and the faster it festers, but if we take it to Christ in prayer, we receive our needed relief. The very act of presenting it to Christ inspires hope and teaches us to be deeply compassionate as well. True compassion changes the way we live. In 1John 4:20, Bible says 'whoever claims to love God yet hates a brother or sister is a liar. For whoever does not love their brother or sister whom they have seen, cannot love God, whom they have not seen.' This tells us that our brother or sister is bound to hurt us to the point where we just want to hate them. However, we cannot continue to pledge allegiance to God every day and hate our offenders. A mark of a true Christian is one who adorns him or herself with the mantle of compassion. We may suffer the injury of our offenders, but we also suffer their sins with them. When Jesus asked God the Father to 'forgive them for they do not know what they do,' He had picked up the burden of their sin on to Himself. These offenders were probably oblivious to the great load of sin that they were carrying. They were also unaware that they had become miserable wretches because they were bound to be thrown to their tormentors. What they needed was a good confession and repentance. Christ made that provision for them, if only they would rise and take it. That is the work of compassion, love and forgiveness.

We also apply the components of compassion in our most desolate periods. We are moved by the action of the sin against us, just as the father in our parable was. We spring into action and run towards our offender, just as the prodigal's father did. We do so by seeing the sin for what it is, and we embrace our offender, having separated their crime from them. This does not have to be a physical embrace, but the act of releasing them from their sin, or caring for the wounded man as the Samaritan did or providing healing, feeding the hungry and forgiving sins as Jesus did. Compassion, gratitude and love are therefore how we are identified as Christ's true disciples, for without that we are nothing but clanging cymbals.

Friend, let us learn to be compassionate in our daily living. It will propel us to stand ready to enfold all our forgiven offenders. We end this portion with scripture from Psalm 103:8-10 which says 'The Lord is compassionate and gracious, slow to anger, abounding in love. He will not always accuse, nor will He harbor His anger forever; He does not treat us as our sins deserve or repay us according to our iniquities.' We also pledge then, not to accuse our offender nor harbor the anger of their sin forever. We will not treat them as their sins may deserve, because we really do not know the cost of justice. We will abound in love and allow God to work His mercy through us. Amen.

CHAPTER 11
TAKE THAT STEP

It is so important that we take great strides to forgive everyone who hurts us. The reasons have been adequately explained, but this point is so essential that it bears repeating over and over. You see, pain caused by an offender is very difficult to deal with and the only sure way of getting over that pain is to take the bold step of forgiveness. We need to continue to remind ourselves of the need to forgive quickly when sinned against so that we do not hold grudges in our hearts. It is important to remind readers that forgiveness is not really us doing the offender a favor. It is us doing ourselves the biggest favor we can possibly do for self. Whenever the Holy Spirit reminds us of the tiniest grudge that is fast building in our hearts, we must do well to tend to it immediately. We reverse our bitterness, misery and pain, with bigger portions of joy and peace and the knowledge that we have pleased God, and there is rejoicing in Heaven. I encourage all of us to make that worthy decision every day to have a heart of forgiveness always. Do not hesitate at all. To the best of your ability, just begin the process of forgiveness immediately.

When we refer to our parable, the father was in great expectation, eager, and waiting diligently to forgive his son in person. He had already done the FOR part of forgiving. Remember our definitions in chapter one? Heaven was rejoicing because he had freed his heart, and at the sight of repentance coming across the field towards him, the GIVE part was fulfilled. He immediately, without hesitation ran towards his son to be reconciled. To For-Give is both a spiritual and physical endeavor – first we do so deep in our heart with prayer, then we complete it - where possible - in the flesh with prayer. We may still be confused, heartbroken, and may even suffer the consequences of the sin. We may also be in pain, but we still must work hard on the 'FOR'. We will be cleansed, and when the time is right, God will help us to finish the GIVE part of the process. Friend, do not therefore despair if you have yearned to forgive an offender both in your heart and in person, but have failed to achieve the GIVE (reconciliation) portion. As long as you have worked on the FOR portion, that is, your heart has been cleared of that load, you have forgiven. While working hard towards the reconciliation portion, do not beat yourself up if it is not happening fast enough. Leave it in God's hands. When possible or necessary, the entire process will be fulfilled to His glory.

I. Alter at the Altar
'And when you stand praying, if you hold something against anyone, forgive them, so that your Father in Heaven may forgive you your sin.' - Mark 11:25
 We may be carrying out what we think is the most noble act, immersed in a time of fragrant worship unto God. Suddenly, the Holy Spirit nudges us about our feelings of resentment against another person. We brush this thought aside and say to ourselves, 'this is not such a big deal, let me just continue with this wonderful time of prayer.' Or we may slip in a quick 'God forgive me' and continue with the worship session. Jesus says succinctly, that our time of worship means nothing if we hold a grudge against our brother or sister. Clearly, we have perfected the art of sorting offenses according to person and size of sin as we see it. We are thus able to attempt forgiveness of some sins and hold the big ones hidden in our hearts, leaving them to fester. Jesus chooses what we consider our most noteworthy pursuit to tell us that we are wasting our time if there is even a bit of unforgiveness in our hearts. Our Father in Heaven will not heed our noble fragrant prayers if

they are laced with grudges. Our duty is to forgive our offenders, Jesus is saying, and this must never be a half-hearted or fake effort. If we hold something against anyone, we must immediately stop the prayer and rectify the situation first. This verse tells us how important forgiveness and reconciliation are to Jesus. We may argue that what can be better than spending time with God in praise and worship? Nothing, we may think, should interrupt this noble act.

Jesus says alter your thoughts and actions at the altar. We are admonished to take the right step of forgiveness. This verse also reminds us that forgiveness is a spiritual process of the heart and we must never hesitate to obediently listen out for any anomalies and correct them. As we pray therefore, we change course as the Holy Spirit directs, and search our hearts for any inkling of unforgiveness. Once located, we release the offender immediately and continue with our prayers. This process is imperative because our prayers will suddenly take on new meaning. Our Father in Heaven will notice that our hearts are no longer burdened and will forgive us for our sins as well. When the Holy Spirit reminds us to forgive as we stand to pray, there should be no argument. We must be quick to respond to this reminder. It is not a time to appraise the size and depth of the sins against us. Take that quick step and release the debt. The father in our story took his own steps to make peace with his lost son deep within his heart. He had spent long moments in prayer, and the verse in Mark 11 above always touched a spot in him. He knew the importance of releasing the sin from his son so that the prospect of reconciliation would be fulfilled. He often hoped that his older son would be of the same mind, spend more time in prayer and forgive his younger brother for all the grief he had put them through. The malicious words and spiteful language of his older son towards his brother was a great concern to him. He trusted that a time would come that there would be no thoughts of revenge against his younger brother. He would, in the meantime continue his vigil up on his roof-top. Reader, once we forgive, we let go of all resentment, and our own forgiveness is granted by God, in prior response to our repentance. Then our prayers will rise up like a sweet-smelling incense unto the Lord. Our goal at all times is always to pause at the altar to check if we need to alter the direction of our prayers. We must endeavor to be decisive in taking that step towards forgiveness and possible reconciliation at all times. It pleases God.

II. Leave that Gift
'Therefore, if you are offering your gift at the altar and there remember that your brother or sister has something against you, leave your gift there in front of the altar. First go and be reconciled to them; then come and offer your gift.'
- Matthew 5: 23-24

Once again, we are engrossed in our considered noble act of offering a gift at the altar of God. A well thought of gift, possibly presented with many other benevolent acts to our local church complemented with a time of fasting to enrich the process. We feel very pious and satisfied that our 'works of the law' – Romans 9:32, have placed us in God's good books. Yet Jesus is not impressed at all because we have unconfessed sins in our hearts against a brother or sister. If we are offering our gift at the altar, and there remember that we offended someone, Jesus asks that we go seek forgiveness and reconciliation first before we continue with our benevolent acts and gift giving. In other words, our generous gift loses its import if we have not pursued forgiveness and reconciliation.

The priceless well thought of gift suddenly becomes a worthless piece of garbage that no one has use for, if we have not sought forgiveness from those we wounded. Holy Spirit our counsellor and friend is sure to remind us, time and again that there is rancor in our heart, or there are sins that need desperate repentance. Stop everything and deal with those first. Leave your gift, Jesus says. It is of no value if we need forgiveness. The gift means nothing if a victim harbors resentment against us. Clear out your heart first, Christ says, yearn for harmony, He admonishes, go make peace with your neighbor! We ought to desire and seek reconciliation with our brother and sister at all costs, then we can come back to the business of gift giving and see how God will honor us.

In our parable story of the lost son, both father and younger son show remarkable grace as they take steps towards forgiveness and reconciliation. The younger son says in Luke 15:18 that 'I will set out and go back to my father and say to him: Father, I have sinned against Heaven and against you. Taking the step towards repentance and reconciliation is not easy. One must determine in one's heart, hear the voice of the Holy Spirit, be emboldened, confident and ready. Imagine the humiliation the younger son could have felt at the thought of going back home completely humbled. His servants, friends, older brother, father would all have their opinions on his bad behavior. His older brother especially, gave him pause for thought. The disdain that emanated when he dared share with him his plan to abscond with his share of the inheritance had been a sore point of contention. Now however, he had to ignore all those thoughts and take the step – in pursuit of forgiveness. He was determined to make this move because of the goodness of God. He was moved by the verse above from Matthew 5:23-24. What good did it do him to build a wedge between himself and his family? He was grateful to God for this chance to take the step back home and make things right. Pride was out of the window, and humility had come in through the door.

Friend, we must take the bold steps to forgive and be forgiven. It is worthier than offering a gift at the altar. It is worthier than standing to pray at the altar. Heal the heart first, Jesus says, and then get on with all other things. We humbly pray that God will help us in our quest to remain forgiven and pass it on always.

III: Seeking Forgiveness
'Blessed is the one whose transgressions are forgiven, whose sins are covered.' - Psalm 32:1

In the parable of the unforgiving servant found in Matthew 18:21-35 this wicked servant lost his reservation to Heaven because he did not have a heart of forgiveness. As such, he could neither seek nor extend forgiveness sincerely. He was not contrite nor repentant over his own debts nor did he feel compassion for his fellow servant for a smaller debt. It is an inherent human characteristic to feel the need to extend forgiveness when affronted, and likewise, we were intrinsically created to recognize the need to seek forgiveness when we trespass against our neighbor. Yet because of our fallen nature, if we do not work on these gracious natural attributes, we lose the knack of its application, causing us to work our way towards our tormentor's camp. Our hearts become hardened and we may go through the motions of repentance or extending forgiveness, but it may never be real.

This wicked servant was just going through life with a hardened heart, unwilling to deal with the requirements of forgiveness. Maybe, he forgot that everyone confronts forgiveness in one form or another as part of life's basic order, so when his master charged him and his family to be sold to repay his debt, he knew to fall to his knees before the master and beg for patience. Matthew 18:26. The master was compassionate and canceled the entire debt but the remorse shown by the servant had been feigned. It was a farce. He could not value the significance of what had just happened to him, because he never had it in his heart to cultivate the principles of forgiveness anyway. Much as he went through the motions of contrition and remorse, he had an unforgiving heart. But you cannot mock God, for He knows every heart and understands all motives. Do we recognize ourselves in this servant? Do we go through the motions of pursuing forgiveness just to get our victims off our backs? Do we comprehend the danger of not seeking forgiveness when we hurt someone? In our Luke 15:11-32 parable study, we find the same contempt for forgiveness in the older brother. In his case, he does not believe he needs it. He is resentful of his younger brother and father for a variety of reasons. This older son believed the world should revolve around him. He was hardworking, pious, always doing all of his father's bidding. He got along with all the servants and people in the city. He never asked for an extra dime, and would not dare ask his father for a young goat to kill and feast with his friends let alone his portion of the inheritance. Why would he ever seek forgiveness? Yet he needed forgiveness for his pride and ego. He needed a Savior to direct his emotions towards love for his family. Not so, the younger son in our story. In Luke 15:18 he said 'I will set out and go back to my father and say to him: Father, I have sinned against Heaven and against you.' This young son had recognized his needy state as was prompted by the Holy Spirit, and sought forgiveness.

We need to seek forgiveness because we have all sinned and fallen short of the glory of God – Romans 3:23. 'There is no one who is good.' – Romans 3:12b It is impossible to make it to Heaven if we do not repent of our sins. Let me repeat that it is impossible to enter the kingdom of God with a load of sin, and an unforgiving heart. The prodigal son in our parable story has shown us how to seek forgiveness. Oftentimes we are gently encouraged by the Holy Spirit when we sin, to seek forgiveness. It is urgent that we hear this call and confess, repent and seek forgiveness as soon as possible, for if we confess, God is faithful and just to forgive us our sins and cleanse us from all unrighteousness – 1John 1:9. Like the prodigal son therefore, we must reflect on our sin, be outraged by its ugliness and overwhelmed and saddened by it. Then comes contrition and brokenness that we flaunt God's law the way we do. The wicked servant's contrition was fake, but the prodigal son cried over his sins, broken and weak. We ought to come to ourselves and rise up to lift our sins to the Lord in tears and trepidation, hating the very idea that we sinned against our God. Now, we boldly turn around, with humility to seek our God again and live a changed life. Then as we live our lives free from sin, we commit daily to God our desire to live for Him. With the help of the Holy Spirit, we live a changed life of purity, humility and joy. It is our prayer that we come to our senses, like the prodigal son did, when we are called to seek forgiveness. The lesson here is that the one forgiven much should forgive greatly too. Grace should be without limit, for God's grace upon us is limitless. May God give us the grace to confess and repent of our sins to Him always and with a smile on our faces and a spring in our step, we too can declare that we are forgiven beings by the grace of God.

IV. Extending Forgiveness
'If you forgive anyone's sins, their sins are forgiven; if you do not forgive them, they are not forgiven.' - John 20:23

The reason to extend or grant forgiveness to our brothers and sisters is to free our hearts from the pain and bitterness that the hurt brings, and work towards reconciliation since this is the will of God. Our goal is to be like Jesus, who forgives unconditionally. He is the perfect model of compassion, humility and forgiveness. We yearn to be holy as God is Holy and to live in peace with everyone as far as it depends on us. Using our favorite story, the parable of the Lost Son, we will continue to examine how we can also effectively extend forgiveness. The father, after hearing the devastating news from his younger son about wanting his share of the inheritance, gathered his composure and did his son's bidding. He acknowledged the pain, but did not hit back. Instead, he went up to his roof-top and held vigil for his son by praying. He tried to identify what caused him the most pain – was it the insolent audacity or the idea that this boy did not want to have a relationship with him? This father tried to understand the wickedness by putting himself into his son's shoes. Had he neglected his boys too much, was peer pressure the problem? The father quickly turned his mind on how far he had come himself. He recognized that he himself was a sinner in need of forgiveness too. Boy, had he wronged God and many people in his lifetime. He was not blameless before God, so as he reflected on how much God had forgiven him, gratitude filled his heart. 'God's forgiveness is made even more precious when you forgive' he said to himself. He thought of the Bible verse in Matthew 7:12 that says 'do unto others what you would have them do to you.' He would surely want everyone to forgive him if he caused them pain, he thought. He held nothing against his younger son but love. This helped him to let go of the pain and push on in prayer. Much as his human mind wanted to curse out his son, this father decided to leave the administration of justice to God. 'It is mine to avenge; I will repay, says the Lord.' – Romans 12:19 So this father would just continue to pray every day for his son, because God knows best and God loves best he thought to himself. With a somewhat reflective demeanor, he sighed with joy and peered into the horizon to catch a glimpse of his son.

That is how we do it friend. We can hardly breathe from the stinging anguish of the sin against us, yet our reaction must be one of perfect composure, to the best of our abilities, with the Holy Spirit holding us close as we endure the horrible pain. We look back at the sin and the sinner, trying to understand how and why it happened, putting it into the best perspective that we can possibly place it in. Yet we do not dwell on it, because we have work to do with the problem. We remember Luke 11:14, that if we hold anything against anyone, to forgive them. We thus lift the person up to God in prayer. God knows how best to deal with sins. He washes them away in the blood of Jesus that was shed on the cross at Calvary. We release the venom from our hearts in its entirety as we continue to pray for our offender. We have come far, we reflect. If God has forgiven us for all our sins when we cried out in repentance, then we too can forgive just as He did us. We are grateful for the opportunity to tell God that we too are forgiving because He forgave us through the blood of Jesus. How joyful it is to know we can take it all to the Lord in prayer. With smiles on our faces and a spring in our step, we declare that we are forgiving beings by the grace of God.

CHAPTER 12
MAKE THE CONNECTION

It is no exaggeration that building a loving relationship with God and with our brothers and sisters is a 'must do' top priority for humanity. This is because a love relationship is so important to God, and we see it commanded one way or another throughout the Bible. In Deuteronomy 6:5 the Bible says 'Love the Lord your God with all your heart and with all your soul and with all your strength,' and in verse 7, it says to impress this commandment to our children. To the question of which the greatest commandment in the law is, Jesus answered 'Love the Lord your God with all your heart and with all your soul and with all your mind. This is the first and greatest commandment and the second is like it: Love your neighbor as yourself, All the prophets hang on these two commandments.' – Matthew 22:37-40 These commandments reveal the magnitude of God's position on love because He is the very essence of love, and is bent on ensuring that its excellence reigns supreme. In 1John 5:2, the Bible says 'This is how we know that we love the children of God: by loving God and carrying out His commands.' It is not far-fetched to appreciate the fact that God is all about restoring relationships because of His love for mankind. Christ then teaches us not to count men's sins against them, but to work at reconciling with our offenders, because God already did this with us. His love and mercy create a path to reconciliation and restoration. If we hear His word and repent of our sins, He restores us to new life. He re-connects us to Himself. The goal here is to look at examples of biblical reconciliations, the effort it took to forgive and reconcile, the joyful effects of reconciliation, and what we can learn from these examples. We will take a look at how depends on us, if it is possible, let us live in peace with everyone.' – Romans 12:18

II. Jacob and Esau
'But Esau ran to meet Jacob and embraced him; he threw his arms around his neck and kissed him. And they wept.'
- Genesis 33:4

This is a remarkable story of how two brothers after years of enmity, came together again and made the connection. We have a lot to learn from this deep rivalry between siblings and how we can, with God's help forgive and reconcile with our brothers and sisters. Earlier in their lives, Jacob had tricked his brother Esau into selling his birthright over a pot of stew, and later, with the help of his mother, tricked their father Isaac into receiving blessings reserved for Esau. Esau brims with hatred for a long time swearing to kill his brother Jacob. Genesis 27:41 says 'Esau held a grudge against Jacob because of the blessing his father had given him. He said to himself, "the days of mourning for my father are near; then I will kill my brother Jacob."' There was a deep hatred and bitterness on Esau's side which sent Jacob into exile. Being an offender can sometimes be lonely and cold. Jacob found out the hard way the effects of his deceptions. Afraid, lonely and defenseless while in exile, Jacob was positioned to hear from God. We are reminded of the prodigal son in our parable, as he lay in the pig-pen, waiting for God to speak to his heart. A deep humility came over the prodigal son in that period of desolation and Jacob displayed same which is what may happen to us in order to get that reconciliation going with our victim or offender. Jacob, was assured of God's providence, comfort and counsel, and from that moment, he forgave himself, and sought God's forgiveness as well. He was ready to make the connection with his brother.

God had worked on Jacob's heart, and He commanded him to reconcile with his brother. Genesis 31:3 says 'Then the Lord said to Jacob, "go back to the land of your fathers and to your relatives, and I will be with you."' With fear and trepidation but determined to reconcile with his brother, Jacob places his trust in God and heads back home to Esau. Genesis 32:11 shows us that Jacob is just as human as we are, 'save me,' he prays, 'from my brother Esau, for I am afraid he will come and attack me.' Yet he is unwavering in his decision to heed God's command to make the connection with his brother. We see here that the connection begins with God, Genesis 32:1, so whenever we enter His presence He reveals our brokenness and prompts us to reconcile with the offended party. Whatever God lays on our hearts to do, in order to make the connection is what must be of interest to us. May God always give us the strength to be obedient to His Word as we seek to repair our relationships. In Genesis 32:25, Jacob wrestled with God, who injured His hip in return for a blessing. When we are determined to reconcile with our victim or our offender for that matter, it may take everything we have. We will struggle with God and humans, but God will always be with us, because He yearns for that connection of peace to ensue.

Friend, making a reconciliation connection is not easy, but with God's help, we must determine to do so. It involves faith, sacrifice, risk, sometimes injury and most certainly trust. With all that effort comes growth and a deeper connection with God. Since God has reconciled us to Himself through Jesus Christ, we can reconcile with one other, no longer counting our offenses against each other. This desire must be well thought of, prayed about and deliberately executed. We see Jacob sending specific messages and greetings to his brother as he plans his journey back home. Genesis 32:3-5. Let us also take the initiative as Jacob did, stay in prayer like he did and humble ourselves like he did. This attitude puts us in a position for reconciliation to occur because our vulnerability allows God to work through us towards our brothers and sisters. From this story, we learn that forgiveness can change history's setting, as it did with Jacob. We can also be an instrument of change in the kingdom of God if we avail ourselves to forgiveness and reconciliation.

III. Joseph Forgives his Brothers
'Then Joseph said to his brothers, "Come close to me." When they had done so, he said, "I am your brother Joseph, the one you sold into Egypt! And now, do not be distressed and do not be angry with yourselves for selling me here, because it was to save lives that God sent me ahead of you."' - Genesis 45: 4-5

There is a very poignant story in Genesis 45 about Joseph and his brothers – where a painful breach in relationship is confronted and resolved. Joseph was greatly favored by his father Jacob over his other brothers causing great resentment and jealousy throughout his life with them. Joseph revealed a dream to his family that he would be exalted above them and this caused him to be sold into slavery by his brothers. He later endured prison in Egypt, but kept a loving relationship with God despite his woes. We learn that he was granted a high position in Egypt and God used him to save his brothers, fathers and the entire nation of Israel. What makes this story great is just how Joseph went all out to reconcile with his brothers and let grace and forgiveness win out when the opportunity came. Joseph showed his emotions openly and hugged and cried with his brothers as he reconnected with them. He showed kindness and love, and there were certainly no thoughts of revenge and bitterness. He portrayed the components of compassion, by relying on the promptings of God and submitting totally to Him. Joseph exhibited great grace and generosity of heart which is always important when reconciling with one who has previously hurt us. Making a good connection has to do with our renewed restored outlook – where there was hatred, cruelty and blame, now there is love, kindness and care. This is the same initiative that we have to take as we stand ready to enfold. As we make the connection with our offenders, it is up to us to apply the love of God, by letting go of anger, bitterness and hostility.

This reconciliation story is important because we are being taught to disregard what our offender has done. In an effort not to let the hurt fester, we do not go back to the details of the sin. As we admonish the offender in the process of reconciliation, we face the sin, but leave the painful analysis to a minimum, so that bitterness will not ensue. As Joseph did, we too must understand and trust that God is sovereign over every circumstance of all life. Joseph did not resign himself to being a victim of fate. He understood that it was God who governs us according to the purpose of His will. God's sovereignty brings us the enablement and comfort to connect with others by looking past their actions and only to God's workings. We can look at every circumstance in our lives and know that it fits into God's eternal purposes and it is an opportunity for us to grow closer to Him. Also, bitterness is a root according to Hebrews 12:15, and like all roots, can take a deep hold if not taken out. Our moment of reconnecting must also be done with trust and God-centeredness. This is because our own strength and wisdom will never permit us to forgive and reconcile with our offenders. It is all the doing of the Lord, so we must apply trust and have Him in the middle of the negotiation so that it ends well. A make-the-connection process is indeed a negotiation process because our offender may be wary of our reasons for wanting to reconcile. Are we doing this to retaliate? The brothers of Joseph were certainly afraid of this man who claimed to be their brother, and it would not have come as a big surprise if they attempted some other horrible sin against Joseph again. It was important that Joseph acknowledged God's sovereignty and superiority throughout the reconciliation process. 'Am I in God's place?' he asked in Genesis 50:19 as he explained to his brothers that God had sent him ahead to preserve their lives from the severe famine that the country was facing. Joseph assured his brothers that he was not angry, and reminded them of God's plan of saving them. These words are an example for us to look at things that happen in our lives always from God's perspective. We do not know why some things happen but if God has allowed it, then He has a purpose for them. As such, if we are looking from God's viewpoint then we can forgive those who hurt us, because God is always working His purpose out to our benefit.

This reconciliation process also highlights another feature, which is obedience. Joseph was waiting for this time from the beginning because he believed that God had a good reason for sending him ahead of his family. Friend, no matter how difficult it may seem, or how neglected we think we are from God, or how painful the offense, the importance of forgiveness, reconciliation and restoration is always on God's heart for us. Regardless of the event in our lives, we must resolve in our hearts to stand firm in obedience. See this through, forgive and go on to reconcile if possible. We never know what God is using the incident for. So, even though we do not know for sure if the brothers ever apologized formally to Joseph or not, he was ready: a changed outlook, compassion, trust in God, boldness and generosity. This is standing ready — it makes you able to enfold your offenders long before you even reach the point of reconciliation. And this is what forgiveness truly looks like.

When someone wrongs us, we must remember this story about Joseph and his brothers. God may have allowed your wound for a very good reason, which we may not know at the time. After all, 'all things work together for good to them that love the Lord.'- Romans 8:28 Therefore, if we have a loving relationship with God and if we have mourned over our own sins and we remember that Jesus died for our sins, and if we have right standing based on all that, we can rest assured that our connection may motivate our offender to deal with his own repentance and turn to be restored by God. Joseph forgave long before he reconciled. He was standing ready to enfold his brothers, as such bitterness could not fester and that should be our goal too. From a contemporary point of view, Joseph could have stewed in anger, re-living the painful details of the events caused by his brothers. He could have met up with other prisoners and planned a revenge scheme on anyone who had a part to play in his supposed demise. His anger could have soared to unimaginable heights and ignited into an explosion so immense that the future of Israel would never have ensued. Nevertheless, Joseph recognized, respected and regarded God every single day. He had presented his sufferings, pain and trials to the Almighty thus a calmness was upon him.

Friend, whenever we have a load of problems, let us pause to ask ourselves if we have told God about them. If the answer is a resounding Yes, we can relax and go about our day. Our sovereign God has a mighty plan for us. Joseph yearned for this reconciliation and reversal of sin, and it eventually happened joyfully. It must be foremost on our minds and in our hearts that God pre-arranged the forgiveness of our sins way before repentance, yet restoration remains un-extended because there can be no reconciliation between Him and sinners until repentance takes place. Since we are to forgive as forgiven, we must always do so, and stand ready to enfold, as the opportunity presents itself by God. But like Joseph and the father in our parable, we must be on the lookout, always ready, listening out for the Holy Spirit who will enable us to release the sin ahead of time. Then we look for opportunities to be kind to our offender so that it may lead him to repentance – Romans 2:4. Let us model God's love and forgiveness and allow Him to use us as agents of reconciliation towards our offenders and we will know the joy of a restored loving God-centered relationship. Make the connection.

IV. The Parable of the Lost Son
'So he got up and went to his father. But while he was still a long way off, his father saw him and was filled with compassion for him; he ran to his son, threw his arms around him and kissed him.' - Luke 15:20

So much has been learned from this parable that Jesus told to his disciples, the Pharisees and Scribes on forgiveness and reconciliation. Notably that, forgiveness is a heart matter and must be pursued or extended quickly lest a grudge festers and maligns. The lost son hit rock bottom hard, before he came to his senses and proceeded to repent. Sometimes, God will allow us to go so low as a prerequisite for genuine repentance and a new start. If we wallow in our pig-pens, and refuse to come to our senses, we are bound to be blinded by our unforgiven state, or harbor an unforgiving heart. As we juxtapose life situations of the two brothers, we see two vastly different outcomes emerging. Whereas the younger heeded the stirring of the Holy Spirit and sat up, the older brother thought himself 'holier-than-thou', and would not humble himself. He therefore missed the voice of the Holy Spirit. Self-righteousness has a tendency of hiding an unforgiving heart. The older brother inwardly thought himself better and more deserving of mercy than his younger brother. After all, he did not demean his father by asking for his share of the inheritance. His anger eventually explodes when he no longer has the ability to hide his true feelings when his younger brother returns. Luke 15:28 says 'The older brother became angry and refused to go in. So his father went out and pleaded with him.' He was of the view that this prodigal brother of his had had his way with sinners, never lifting a finger to help in the field, and now he comes back to squander some more? His anger was justified, he thought. However, the make-the-connection move was totally lost on him. Obviously, this man was bound by his unforgiving heart and until he stopped to listen out for the Holy Spirit and release the poison of anger from his heart, he would be in his pig-pen for some time to come, and thrown to his tormentors eventually.

The younger son on the other hand threw himself upon his father's grace and mercy. Yet, it was not just him who was in communication with the Holy Spirit. The father had already been prepared by God to show grace and this is what our Father in Heaven does. He will always show up if we turn back to Him in deep repentance. The younger son acted on his new faith, which we must do also, regardless of what lies ahead, because we know that we serve a merciful God. He will not turn away anyone who comes to Him in faith and trust. This son came with no merit, but just a new-found faith and readiness to accept whatever was requested of him. We learned that we do not need to encounter our offenders physically before we decide to forgive. It is, after all an internal endeavor, a heart affair. The father had extended forgiveness in his heart long before he set eyes on his son again, so when he saw him approach from a long way off, it was to reconcile and bestow compassion and love onto him. A son's faith had yielded a father's love. This further informs us of the essential lessons on reconciliation. Father and son were duly reconciled only after the forgiveness transaction had progressed. Reconciliation after forgiveness is what standing ready to enfold sets out to do. No wonder a big celebration had been prepared to welcome the newly forgiven. 'This brother of yours was dead, and is alive again; he was lost and is found.' – Luke 15:32.

Friend, God also rejoices in the presence of angels when forgiveness has occurred and a connection is made. We must therefore always take steps to ensure that no soil will be left fallow in our garden of forgiveness. That we will make it our aim and goal to go all out to run the forgiveness course all the way towards reconciliation. We will not look back and act like martyrs or heroes which is what some do when they have been victimized, but rather forge on to make a reconciliation connection. It may take time, as it was proving to be with the older son and his father in our story. It may also never happen, but we will forever make that effort. We will determine in our hearts to run as fast as possible, to hug as hard as conceivable so as to make that connection with our offenders, for we do not know the plans of God, and maybe, just maybe, that was God's plan all along, that through us, our offenders may know His saving grace.

PART D
CONCLUSIONS

Yes indeed, life after all, is about relationships. We were created to have a glorious relationship with God and to experience the fruits of His nature and the full effect of His marvelous glory. It is our ability to embrace the power of forgiveness and everything it stands for that gives us the full spectrum of beautiful relationships. Suffice it to say that, society does not frown on a heart that is unforgiving. On the contrary, it encourages us to take matters into our own hands when we suffer an infraction. Views such as 'Let them stew in hell' or 'have nothing to do with that person again' are widely encouraged. 'Be wise,' society goads further, 'stay far away from them.' Dear reader, society is certainly not God's spokesperson and He is not about destroying relationships. He yearns for great relationships that flourish from continuous reconciliation and restoration, and all this will be possible if we, His beloved will receive His forgiveness and extend it too – always. Also, God's wisdom far exceeds human wisdom, so 'being wise' for a Christian means seeking God's wisdom in our forgiveness endeavors. By offering forgiveness, our offender may be receiving the one break they need to repent of their sins and also have a personal relationship with Christ our savior. May God grant us the wisdom to approach forgiveness the same way Jesus did; filled with love, grace, compassion, obedience and gentleness. In this final section therefore, let us recollect and sum up our understanding of the power of forgiveness.

I. God's Perfect Plan
'A life lived without forgiveness is a prison.'
— William Arthur Ward 17

We have established that the phenomenon of forgiveness was created by God, and is a two-way transaction which requires humanity seeking the offer from God while extending it to our offenders. God's perfect plan for forgiveness first came together in the form of Love. It took all of His love to allow His only son die on the cross to save us from our sins. We therefore understand forgiveness in its entirety in the light of the definition of God's love. That forgiveness is truly practical love. If we do not cultivate a heart of forgiveness, we cannot successfully love. Bible says in 1Corinthians 13:1-3 that 'If I speak in the tongues of men or of angels, but do not have love, I am only a resounding gong or a clanging cymbal. If I have the gift of prophecy and can fathom all mysteries and all knowledge, and if I have a faith that can move mountains, but do not have love, I am nothing. If I give all I possess to the poor and give over my body to hardship that I may boast, but do not have love, I gain nothing.' Thus, if we are eloquent and fluent in language, speak with sincerity and charm but our hearts have no love, our speech is just noise and is meaningless. In the same way, if we glow before men, are serviceable and harmonious but bear a grudge against someone who hurt us, our manifestation is fake and does not please God. The outward acts of love and ability will be seen as vain-glory or proud conceit of merit, if love does not abound from within. Now, since forgiveness is love in action, it is important to remember that we may do all the wonderful things on earth, but holding on to a grudge, however tiny, cancels out the good we do. It is the letting go or our willingness to forgive that is acceptable to God. Our ability to love is deepened when we practice forgiveness, and we tend to forgive more quickly when we understand this love connection of Calvary. 'For God so loved the world that he gave his only begotten son, that whosoever believeth in him should not perish but have eternal life.' – John 3:16 Do you remember our definitions of forgiveness in Chapter One? Giving before the incident? Love gives and shares, and that is what forgiveness does too. The test of love is how freely we forgive. This love is between us and God first. When God gave Jesus, He was saying 'I love you so I give you forgiveness' – that is the divine expression of love. If God can love us by forgiving our transgressions, then it stands to reason that we also must love by forgiving. Love gives and true love forgives, it is said. As such, forgiveness is love being demonstrated. John 15:12 says 'love each other as I have loved you,' and John 13:34 says 'a new command I give you: love one another.' Jesus adequately demonstrated this love by His act of dying for us. He did not stop to analyze the effects of our wrongdoings, nor make the sinful things we had done fester in His heart. He immediately acted on His love by forgiving us. That is a very deep fact of forgiveness. The ability to turn the hurt around by looking squarely at that which God gave. If we are devoid of the power to forgive, then we are devoid of the power to love because the highest form of love is forgiveness.

Secondly, God's perfect plan for forgiveness came together through His Grace, of which there is no limit. We thank God for this costly grace which He freely lavishes on us. He supplies the needs of each of us every day because His grace is boundless and sufficient. 2Corinthians 12:9 says 'My grace is sufficient for you, for my power is made perfect in weakness.' Grace does not contemplate if a feat will be beneficial to God or not. The grace favor does not wait nor does it calculate, but runs towards an adversary with a mind only to forgive and to save. When we rely totally on the grace of God, we can turn the hurts done us around and show forgiveness. Grace allows transformation to take place within us. Revelations 1:5b defines what God's grace did for us – 'He loved us and freed us from our sins by His blood,' and because of this grace of God, our sins are totally blotted out the moment our faith activates contrition and repentance. By one sacrifice on the cross, there is remission of sin. Our redemption is complete through the blood of Jesus. Forgiveness granted by grace is the only way not to be taken hostage by the ugly past but have our hope and confidence restored. It is the only way to give all our relationships the blessing of new beginnings. We should therefore always be motivated by the power of divine grace which is in Christ Jesus. He lifts us up when we are down, and helps us to move on in times of difficulty. This grace though invisible, coaxes us away from fear, anxiety and shame and drives us towards repentance and reconciliation and a fresh start. So, is it not wonderful to know that we have not only been called to forgive, but we have also been graced with everything we need to answer this call? As we decide in our minds to let forgiveness manifest always in our life, let us invite Christ daily to work on our hearts, to enlighten us with the understanding that we need to fully forgive from our hearts and to always be open to that choice, for there is no greater peace than knowing that all our sins are forgiven because of grace. We can now enjoy access into God's holy presence. We have no fear of our tormentors because of the grace atonement by the blood of Jesus.

Thirdly, forgiveness as part of God's perfect plan deals with Infinity. When Peter asked Jesus how many times he ought to forgive his offender, Jesus answered in Matthew 18:22 'I tell you, not seven times, but seventy times seven.' By now we have figured out that forgiveness should be never-ending! Infinite, Limitless! Always! We do not keep score and we do not keep count, we just get into the habit of continuous forgiveness. This is what Jesus preached. We must live in perpetual forgiveness, whether we seek or extend it. Jesus used the parable of the wicked servant in Matthew 18:21-35 to explain why forgiveness must be immeasurable. The wicked servant in this parable harbored a spirit of unforgiveness, which made his walk with God inevitably nonexistent. As such, he missed out on all the benefits of forgiveness when he blocked the cycle of debt release. When forgiveness is finite for us, resentment, hate, grudges and the like continue to make their home in our hearts and cause us emotional, physical and spiritual pain. In that case, even when we seek forgiveness, there is no contrition and we are unable to pass on this good gesture. The wicked servant did not understand the continuity that forgiveness requires, thus could not bring himself to pass it on. He was enslaved by unforgiveness. Matthew 18:35 says 'This is how my Heavenly Father will treat each of you unless you learn to forgive your brother from your heart.' We may all start out like the unforgiving servant, coming before God with many sins and begging for His forgiveness and because He is rich in mercy, God quickly pardons us through the blood of Jesus and sets us free. Yet, we harbor a grudge so deep and so big in our hearts against our offenders and because of our egos, we cannot look past the pain and hurt. Then when we suffer from migraine headaches, stress, incessant worry and the like, we tend to blame the devil. No, it is simply a bad case of an unforgiving heart for which the prescription is always seventy-seven times seven. The application of this story remains the same for us. We must continually release pain and anger as they come, so there is no buildup of hatred within us. God's love and grace upon us is beyond our comprehension and it is our ad-infinitum seeking for and granting of forgiveness that preserves us from the torments of sin. Let us allow this love and grace to flow always, as His perfect plan unfolds in our lives.

II. The Joy of Forgiveness
'Restore to me the joy of Your salvation and grant me a willing spirit, to sustain me.' - Psalm 51:12

If you have not experienced the joy associated with becoming a forgiven human being and a champion at forgiving others by the grace of God, then yearn to be so, for it is a liberating feeling. To reach the joyous heights that forgiveness offers, we constantly ought to search our hearts and minds and let Holy Spirit reveal any bitterness stuck in there, then confess, repent and get them out of the way. This is what we have to do on a continual basis as we consider the price Christ paid on the cross at Calvary. Doing this is also the sure way of increasing our faith as well as motivating us to be more like Christ. Then as our hearts lighten, we receive an earthly picture of the joy Heaven has in store for us. It causes us to be kinder, better able to create a peaceful life and more than anything, we grow in grace. As far as it depends on us, may we move away from the wiles of sin, the bitterness of unforgiveness, and into the realm of joy, serenity, and a closer walk with God. This brings the assurance of God's love and makes us even more determined to love and forgive others by the example of Christ. It further restores our hope for the future because we see beyond the injustices we suffer and we look to the joy forgiveness brings about in our lives. The fattened calf will be served – Luke 15:23, celebrations will begin, there will be loud music and dancing, and in the Heavenly realm also, the angels will rejoice over the repentance of a sinner. All this over a persons' decision to choose forgiveness. What a joy! May God Himself help us treasure the joy of forgiveness and demonstrate it by seeking and granting forgiveness always.

Thus, if you are still tentative about forgiving a terrible infraction against you, I urge you to let it go. 'Get rid of all bitterness, rage and anger, brawling, slander, along with every form of malice. Be kind and compassionate to one another, forgiving each other, just as in Christ God forgave you.' – Ephesians 4:3 Indeed, you may have been through the wringer with a very painful offense, and you cannot even begin to think of forgiveness let alone, the joy it brings. You may be fearful of the unknown should you consider forgiveness, and this could come in the form of fear of losing the energy of your anger against the sinner or fear of repercussions. Yet, as we have learned, forgiveness is topmost in God's vocabulary in the dispensation of love. God introduced forgiveness very early in scripture to teach us how to humbly, peacefully and joyfully get along with everyone. It is true that when we do give the gift of forgiveness, we are sure to receive a wounded heart for the sake of Christ, yet nothing is better than picking up our cross and following Christ all the way. Our ultimate reward is in Heaven. Paul said in James 1:2-4 to 'consider it pure joy, my brothers and sisters, whenever you face trials of many kinds, because you know that the testing of your faith produces perseverance. Let perseverance finish its work so that you may be mature and complete, not lacking anything.'
David, in Psalm 32 describes this joy of forgiveness. 'Blessed is the one whose transgressions are forgiven, whose sins are covered. Blessed is the one whose sin the Lord does not count

against them and in whose spirit is no deceit.' – Psalm 32:1-2 We all stand in need of God's grace and forgiveness because we carry a load of sin before a holy and perfect God. This Psalm describes how anguish caused by sin can turn into great joy by taking it to God. 'When I kept silent, my bones wasted away through my groaning all day long. For day and night your hand was heavy on me; my strength was sapped as in the heat of summer.' Psalm 32:3-4 Yet in verse eleven the psalmist says 'Rejoice in the Lord and be glad, you righteous; sing, all you who are upright in heart!' This is the joy we experience when our sins are taken away, and we are made righteous by the blood of Jesus. The prodigal son blinked in amazement when the 'scales fell off his eyes,' and he realized that he could go home. When he found out that his destiny was not in the form of pods from a pig-pen, but rather the choicest of meats in his father's home, he was filled with joy. There was joy in his heart when he knew without a shadow of doubt that he had received forgiveness. His father experienced a similar joy when he saw his son approaching, and with outstretched arms, they reconciled and danced a joyful dance. Friend, rejoice in the Lord for there is pure joy when transgressions have been lifted. You will be unburdened and your joy will be restored. It is worth a try.

III. The parable of the Lost Son
"'My son,' the father said, 'you are always with me, and everything I have is yours. But we had to celebrate and be glad, because this brother of yours was dead and is alive again; he was lost and is found.' - Luke 15:31-32

'My son,' the older brother muttered with disdain. He had not felt like a son to his father in many years. 'Everything you have is mine?' he berated under his breath. He shook his head bitterly even though he could see sincerity in his father's eyes. He just was not ready to believe what he was hearing. He, a son, worked harder than every servant in the household and even then, his hard work never paid off, he scoffed. Not even a young goat to celebrate with his friends, and today father tells him that all he had was his? This older son was in grave danger! He had hardened his heart to all forms of forgiveness. Dear reader, if the enemy will gain ground in destroying our lives as Christians, the spirit of unforgiveness will always be a factor. We go about our merry way with an abundance of unforgiveness weighing down our hearts yet masquerading as normal everyday events. This is when bitterness, resentment, anger and despair are not dealt with appropriately. For the sake of our salvation let us apply all we have learned in The Power of Forgiveness to our daily lives. Do we struggle to seek or grant forgiveness? Who do we have to forgive? A spouse, friend, a stranger, our own selves? It does not matter who. We have to give up that tumor of grief that has weighed us down so long. The angry older brother said to his father, 'But when this son of yours who has squandered your property with prostitutes, comes home, you kill the fattened calf for him!' — Luke 15:30 This son had obviously harbored a load of anger in him and was blinded at the prospect of repentance and seeking forgiveness. If his attitude is familiar to us, let us take cues from this story. We may think of ourselves as good and virtuous because we may not be living a wild lustful life. Yet are we in a distant country of unforgiveness, anger and hatred? We do not have to be in a distant country to squander our life away when we know Christ and His forgiveness. We have to get on our knees and earnestly ask God to forgive us for not forgiving our brother or sister. Jesus Christ has paid the price for all sins with His blood, and this knowledge must propel us to run full speed towards the cross with repentance in our hearts. It takes a touch of the Holy Spirit to come to our senses.

We are now at the end of our journey with Jesus' parable of the Lost Son. We met the long-suffering father, the arrogant but repentant younger son and the self-centered unforgiving older son. What do these characters stand for? The father stands for everything that forgiveness and reconciliation connote. Regardless of the painful sins of both sons, this father did not let that negatively dictate his own actions. The forgiveness process started in his heart long before the prodigal's return, and long before his older son's angry outbursts. He acts out his love when he runs full speed to embrace his younger son, and he also lovingly tells his older son that he is with him always. He stared at the sins, but always chose to be obedient to God, for he himself enjoyed being forgiven by God and he knew the benefits. He used the process of reconciliation to assure the lost son of his desire to bring him into his fold again. In the same way he expressed his deep love for his older son by reminding him of his enduring grace. No wonder the father said, 'But we had to celebrate.' – Luke 15:32, in his bid to foster reconciliation. This sure is the natural course of events when there is an awakening, and this father stands for great awakenings. We, like the older son in this parable may not want to enter the house of celebration to be awakened. We need an awakening though, and Jesus has done what we cannot do. Through the power of His death and resurrection, He purifies us from sin, 1John 1:7. In Heaven there is rejoicing when the lost is found and so should there be on earth. Yet when we are hemmed in by our bitterness and resentment, we are stifled and cannot grow. We remain unawakened and die in our unforgiveness.

The older brother stands for a heart waiting to be thawed. Yes, he was obedient and hardworking, seeking to submit to all rules in his father's house. Yet he was haughty and thought he could earn God's grace and blessings by his works. He treated salvation like a contract with a quid-pro-quo proviso. 'I work hard then I get a young goat to celebrate with my friends.' We understand from the older son's tone of voice and exchange of words with his father that, the condition of our heart is not revealed by our outward dutiful behavior, but by our inward attitude towards people and God. The older son refused to recognize sin in his heart, so saw no need for forgiveness. By observing his stance, we identify that unforgiveness is a dangerous disease that puts Christians in servitude. It is a very effective method devised by the devil to steal a person's blessings. This son portrays an unforgiving heart that dwells on the sin committed against him, wanting revenge, constantly re-living the sins, and getting more bitter with each passing day. Inevitably, the sin is never separated from the sinner to be placed on the cross of Jesus. The older brother's tone of voice speaks of pride and self-aggrandizement. He has judged himself favorably to himself, and this is not a humble spirit. He self-righteously and arrogantly said to his father in Luke 15:29, 'Look! All these years I've been slaving for you and never disobeyed your orders. Yet you never gave me even a young goat so I could celebrate with my friends.' His service to his father was therefore not out of love, but for what he would get out of it. In short, his unforgiving heart had robbed him of all joy and he was left with a self-piteous, angry and jealous frame of himself. The father, wanting badly to repair the relationship between brothers, counters his older son and says to him, 'This brother of yours was dead and is alive again.' – Luke 15:32 Yet the older son could not fathom this awakening, and felt short-changed by his father for not getting what he thought he deserved. Do you stand for him?

The younger son on the other hand stands for all the possibilities forgiveness has to offer. We learned that after a bout with pride and disobedience this son did come to his senses by the grace of God. He pursued forgiveness vigorously and was rewarded with his father's forgiving embrace. It took a break in his arrogance and a decision to humble himself to make that reconciliation possible. With a keen heart on Holy Spirit's direction, contrition, repentance and a desire to go God's way, this son received the joy and power forgiveness has to offer. He had put his ego aside, and hurried to the safety of his father's arms, where love resided. Do you stand for him?

Dear reader, Jesus has risked everything on that cross just to forgive you and I and reconcile us with our Father too. This is what love does, and it is beautiful in God's eyes. What do we then stand for? Do we identify with any of the characters and activities in the parable? Do we harbor resentment and bitterness in our hearts towards others? Do we deposit the hurt we feel about our offenders with Jesus and have compassion for them? Do we constantly go to God in repentance and confession and seek His forgiveness? Do we forgive ourselves and offenders and seek it from the people we sin against? We learned from our parable that we ought to pursue God's forgiveness with everything we have. We cannot allow the forgiveness work done on the cross to be in vain, and we need that status of 'forgiven', in order to humbly forgive as Christ did. Christ is unhappy when He stands at the door of our hearts and knock and we do not open Him – Revelation 3:20. When that happens, the forgiveness transaction cannot succeed, and like the older son we are unable to confront our sins in contrition and unable to confess, repent and receive the forgiveness we all badly need. We also learned that it is a dangerous thing to mark ourselves as righteous and not seek God's forgiveness in our lives. We learned that reconciliation is a very important part of the forgiveness transaction. Jesus said to go find our offender and rebuke him for his infraction, forgive him and proceed to reconcile when he repents. This tells us that we must stand ready to enfold others at all times for as long as it depends on us, we must live in peace with each other. We did learn that there is joy in reconciliation. With it comes celebration with a fattened calf which is a very far cry from pods in a pig-pen. This is how much God will move to bring us out of the miry clay when forgiveness has occurred. When that happens, our sins no longer separate us from the love of God, because the work of the cross has bridged that gap for us and we stand the best chance of that extraordinary relationship with our Father in Heaven. Moreover, we learned the grim truths about the tragedy of unforgiveness, that it can cripple relationships and destroy one's ability to live a full Christian life. By its very nature, unforgiveness tends to be a blend of pride and ego, which are dangerous tools in the devil's camp! As such, it may be a hard pill to swallow, but it is important to look at our own selves too whenever the need for forgiveness arises. Are pride and ego lurking anywhere nearby, did we contribute to, or go wrong in any way for the sin to occur? Maybe the infraction was totally unprovoked, but either way, as we humble ourselves and keep our eyes on the Lord, the forgiveness wheel can safely turn. It will always certainly be a hard thing to do, but we learned that staring at the sin long and hard and eschewing it helps us to develop the humility needed to send it on its way to the cross rather than harbor it in our hearts. This is what the father in the parable did so admirably. We ought to come to grips with the concept of forgiveness, for if we do not forgive, we walk according to the flesh, and the fruit of the spirit – love, joy, peace, forbearance, kindness, goodness, faithfulness, gentleness and self-control – Galatians 5:22, will not feature fully in our Christian walk.

Finally, we found out that God did not wait for us to approach Him first to extend forgiveness. He did the entire work on the cross, and as long as we come to Him in repentance, we are restored. In Luke 24:46-47 'He told them, "This is what is written: The Messiah will suffer and rise from the dead on the third day, and repentance for the forgiveness of sins will be preached in His name to all nations, beginning at Jerusalem."' Our sins are covered. No more guilt. We are forgiven. Acts 17:27 says 'God did this so that they would seek Him and perhaps reach out for Him and find Him, though He is not far from any one of us.' Since God in His holiness, forgives us of our sins as long as we repent of them, our actions should not hinge on the actions of another. We likewise do not wait for those who offend us to come begging for forgiveness first, but we release the sin immediately so we do not fester a grudge within us. We stand ready to enfold by using all means necessary to persuade repentance, purpose being to regain our brother or sister – Matthew 18:15 says 'If your brother or sister sins, go and point out their fault, just between the two of you. If they listen to you, you have won them over.'

IV: There is Power in Forgiveness
'Blessed are those whose transgressions are forgiven, whose sins are covered. Blessed is the one whose sin the Lord will never count against them.' - Romans 4:7-8

When we keep our eyes on the work of the cross every day and show gratitude for the blood of Jesus that saved and reconciled us to God through His resurrection, our blessings are assured. The power is in our hands! And guess what Reader, Christ's work on the cross is the power behind our power! Christ's power also enables us to quickly stand ready to be reconciled with our offender, after eliminating their sin from our hearts. None of this story will make sense to one who has not experienced the joy of God's forgiveness in Jesus Christ. If we do not forgive as the scriptures command, then the problem is with our ignorance of what God has done for us in Christ Jesus, for Christ sought us on behalf of God to persuade all to repent, 'for the son of Man came to seek and to save the lost.' – Luke 19:10

We also picture this power of forgiveness as a door that opens to God's best. We know that this door is available to all mankind, but has been obscured by pain and scratched by grudges. Just when we think we have found it, it turns out we may still be standing at the gate of anger, pride or resentment. The secret to securing the forgiveness door is to peel our eyes and fix it on Jesus, and see Him as He was on the cross, then in humility, make ourselves small enough to fit in the door, then close it firmly behind us when we enter, by not going back to the sin that caused its need. This is a conscious daily decision that we must all act on. Though the devil will stop at nothing to blind us and cause us not to find this door, remember that it exists, and God's best dwells within. Find the power to forgive. Get God's best. It is worth it.

Dear Friend, it is my hope that I sounded like a severely broken record in my effort to alert you to the dangers of an unforgiving heart. You see, there is no damage from sin that

Jesus cannot totally remove. He is ready to wash away the effects of sin if we repent and confess. We can be freed from our own pig-pens of arrogance, pride and anger if we willingly take this journey through Forgiveness. Permit yourself to look steadily at the sin that broke you so, and release it to Christ and ask Him to do with it as He pleases, then without a backward glance, decide to stand ready to enfold the person who caused it. Our time here on earth is fleeting and we have to use it very wisely. We must strive in our hearts to exercise real forgiveness every day. It will take courage, integrity and strength, but as we pray daily to appropriate our own forgiveness of sin that has been fully purchased and secured for us by the death of Christ Jesus, we can also seek all manner of forgiveness. Micah 6:8 says, 'He has shown you, O mortal, what is good. And what does the Lord require of you? To act justly and to love mercy and to walk humbly with your God.' Much has been said, several scripture verses quoted, many examples given and now the time has come to try forgiveness: The pathway to freedom. May God be our helper.

END NOTES

1.   Alexander Pope Quote: An Essay on criticism, Part II, 1711

2.   Latin perdonare: https://english.stackexchange.com

3.   Greek Aphiemi: https://www.preceptaustin.org

4.   Old English Forgiefan: https://www.etymonline.com

5.   Aramaic Shbakn: http://kuriakon00.tripod.com

6.   Thomas Watson Quote: https://www.christianquotes.info

7.   Joseph M. Scriven – Hymn: https://www.britannica.com

8.   George Herbert Quote: https://quotationpage.com

9.   Fanny Crosby – Hymn: https://www.britannica.com

10.   Greek Paradidomi: http://gospelhall.org/bible

11.   Judson W. Van DeVenter – Hymn: https://en.m.wikipedia.org

12.   Greek Metanoia: https://blueletterbible.org

13.   C. S. Lewis Quote: The Weight of Glory: on Forgiveness.

14.   M. L. King Jr. Quote: https://kinginstitute.stanford.edu, 1962

15.   Mark Twain Quote: https://www.britannica.com

16.   Alan Paton Quote: https://www.thesouthafrican.com

17.   William Arthur Ward Quote: https://sayingimages.com